FLORISTS' REVIEW

101
one-hundred-and-one
GREAT
DISPLAYS

PUBLISHER:	Frances Dudley
EXECUTIVE EDITOR:	Talmage McLaurin, AIFD
AUTHOR:	Glennis Wright
COPY EDITORS	Cynthia Capellari Shelley Urban
PHOTOGRAPHER:	Stephen Smith
FLORAL DESIGN:	Talmage McLaurin, AIFD Bill J. Harper, AIFD, AAF Leroy Miller, AIFD Teresa P. Lanker Gary Wells, AIFD Matt Wood, AIFD
PRODUCTION COORDINATOR:	James Miller, AIFD
ART DIRECTOR AND PROJECT MANAGER:	Ana Maben

Florists' Review's 101 Great Displays with Coordinating Designs
was designed and produced by Florists' Review Enterprises, Inc.,
Topeka, Kansas. www.floristsreview.com

Printed in the United States by Mainline Printing, Topeka, Kansas.

ISBN:	0-9714860-5-0

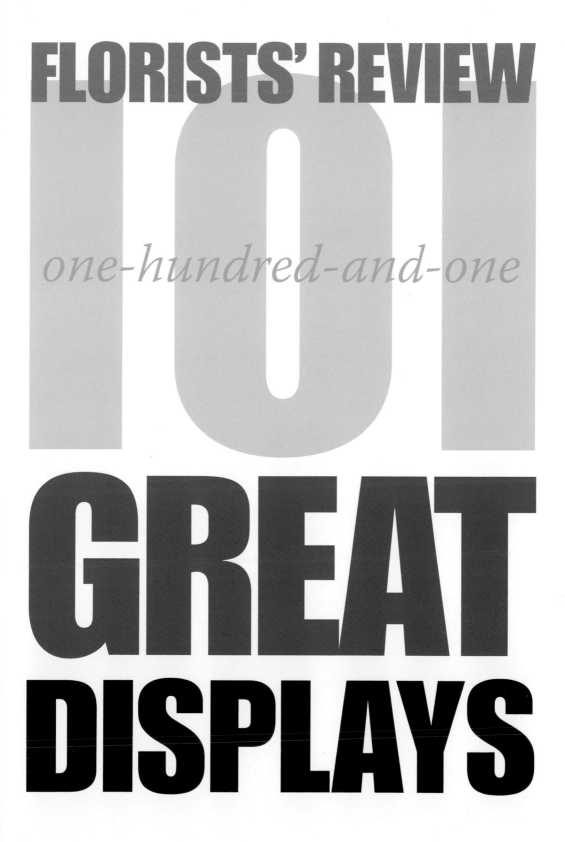

FLORISTS' REVIEW

101

one-hundred-and-one

GREAT
DISPLAYS

introduction

By Glennis G. Wright

How important is the art of display to the success of your shop? Just think, for a moment, about how important sunlight is to growing flowers—that's how necessary it is that merchandise in your store be displayed attractively. When you think about display, you must consider lighting, signage, and how people move when they shop as well as the arrangement of the merchandise. Shopping gives us a chance to freely examine products firsthand. Almost all impulse buying is a result of this sort of shopping opportunity. And that's why merchandising can be as powerful as marketing.

Successful display encompasses many facets, and each should be examined closely. Check the lighting in your window in both natural daylight and at night. Many retail florists don't change the lighting depending on whether it's night or day, which essentially means that visibility in that window isn't optimal during one of those times. Keep in mind, too, that anti-glare film on glass may protect the displayed items from harsh sunlight, but it also makes it hard to see inside the window. It only takes one and a half seconds to walk by a window, so display windows should grab attention from a distance of six feet away.

Whatever is on display in a window must be big and bold, or it's wasted on passersby. They haven't the time to absorb the complete display. Think about how shoppers approach your store and how they move toward your window. According to shopping guru Paco Underhill, people approach your shop almost always from an angle toward the right, which means your display window should be canted to one side to accommodate their line of vision. We walk as we drive—toward the right—so window displays should be tilted to the left. Doing this instantly increases the number of people who really see your display. Something else to think about: if the average shopper visits your store every two weeks, then you should be changing your windows and rotating your interior displays at least that often.

In the pages ahead, you'll find all the inspiration needed to incorporate these ideas into wonderful, easily constructed settings for every season and every holiday—fresh ideas for attractive, effective displays that will increase your profits and make your shop windows and shelves glow with the beauty of flowers year-round.

contents

heart songs

Alive with color, this display makes the heart sing

A joyful display of gregarious red, pale pink, and cream make an emphatic Valentine that literally sings with color. A harlequin doll garbed in holiday red and wearing his heart on his sleeve holds a metal, heart-shaped basket filled with vintage floral postcards and is surrounded by the theme of the romantic holiday. Hearts and a sphere pavéd with permanent velvety red roses and petals, a pot of tall, vibrant red amaryllises and another of soft pink roses add floral notes to this giddy display. A small shelf unit painted in cream provides the foundation and height to back the entire display, and shelves other themed items. Even the shelf could wear a price tag, if you're willing to part with it, since it's small enough to appeal to many customers as a decorative piece.

Vintage papers

Antique papers add a lovely touch to an exuberant clutch of beautiful blossoms for a Valentine presentation. To avoid damaging vintage postcards, which are eminently collectible, make copies with a color copier, and cut heart shapes from the copies, or use decoupage paper with an antique look, easily found at craft stores.

imaginative table skirt

Candles create a spectacular display

An inspired Valentine display showcases a table skirt made of elegantly long, dusty rose taper candles, which are hung from golden upholstery tacks around the edge of the table. On top of the small round table are other candles in two shades of pink and different sizes and shapes interspersed with potted miniature roses. To add vertical height to the display, a hanging heart-shaped wreath made of permanent rose foliage and interwoven with coordinating ribbon complements and completes the display. A perfectly romantic setting for Valentine's Day, the table and its coordinates can easily be adapted to other color palettes and holidays.

1 Cover a table with a table cloth. Hot-glue decorative ribbon trim around the edge of the table.

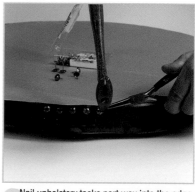

2 Nail upholstery tacks part way into the edge of the table at 1-inch intervals around the edge.

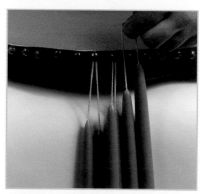

3 Hang pairs of candles by their wicks on the upholstery tacks.

Simplicity shouts

Create this *Gerbera* bud vase by attaching two sections of duct tape, sticky side out, to a cylinder vase. Lily grass (*Liriope*), cut evenly at the bottom of the base, is pressed to the tape to encircle and cover the vase.

visible
valentines

Fresh and affordable
Valentine simplicity

A trio of English boxwood hearts create garden-like valentines for a fresh, new Valentine's Day display. Weathered-looking painted plant frames show two of the hearts at varying levels, and the third is showcased as a topiary in a clay pot. White-washed wooden birds tie the topiary and the plant stands together, and the display is completed with fabric garden roses, arranged with touches of the boxwood, in varying sizes of clay pots. It's a pleasing display that invites attention, simply and effectively.

Embellished bud vase

Explore the possibilities of embellishments for the flower shop staple, the bud vase. All manner of decorative beads, charms, and buttons are available at craft and hobby stores, like the craft store locket used here with a bow of brocaded ribbon. For minimal cost, these smart additions enhance the perceived value of bud vase arrangements and make your designs unique.

homespun valentine

Calico hearts spell Happy Valentine's Day

Swatches of calico fabric found in the quilting department of a local fabric store are cut into traditional heart motifs for inexpensive Valentine's Day décor. The hearts can be cut from fabric using a heart-shaped cookie cutter as a guide, or you can copy an old school room trick of scissoring a heart-shape pattern from a folded piece of paper, cutting the heart to any size you desire. The fabric cutouts are easily attached with spray adhesive to foam-centered board or other surfaces, and the combination of pastels and blues is *so* country. Combine hearts and flowers with blue spatterware and galvanized tin accessories to create a Valentine display that's definitely country!

1 Using a damp sponge, paint a board for a country look.

2 Trace a heart stencil onto fabric and cut out the hearts.

3 Glue fabric to foam-centered board to create the pick, and glue it onto the painted board.

Simply hearts

Simple heart-shaped accessories can help ease the stress of getting ready for the holiday by easily converting a colorful arrangement of vivacious roses and *Cymbidium* orchids into a design that is immediately appropriate for Valentine's Day. Craft foam heart shapes shown here can either be nestled among the blooms or affixed to the container—ours is a planter box that coordinates with the flowers.

country valentine

The simplicity of country style in checked gingham ribbon and hearts

Trace a heart onto a sponge and cut out to create a stencil. Use an acrylic craft paint to stamp the surface of pots and craft paper.

American Country style has withstood the vagaries of fashion and seems destined to continue as an important influence in home decorating and floral design. Hearts have long been a country emblem, and when paired with gingham checked ribbon, they give a fresh, new look to this Valentine arrangement of mini carnations in a heart-stamped terra-cotta pot. The hearts are quickly applied to the pot by using a heart-shaped stamp, which has been dipped in craft paint; the cardboard cutout heart, affixed in the loops of ribbon, adds a little extra bit of "country" flair. For the fantastic craft paper backdrop, simply use the same technique with craft paint and heart-shaped sponges.

Terra-cotta heart

An affordable design is created with a pavé of carnations, arranged in a heart-shaped clay pot. The same idea could be adapted to a spray-painted cardboard heart container, readily available in craft shops, which has been lined with plastic film to keep the container safe from moisture.

old-fashioned charm

An abundance of paper doilies creates delicate designs

Insouciant and fun, paper doilies lend a nostalgic grace to this display. Here we've used the contrast of white and cobalt blue to provide cool balance to the vibrant pinks and reds of roses and *Gerberas*, further sparked by lighter-toned roses. Airy *Gypsophila*, *Astilbe*, and *Statice* in the floral designs emphasize the lacy texture of the doilies. Some of the filigreed rounds are white on a blue background; others are painted blue and placed against stark white. Either way, the paper fantasies create undiluted interest in a vignette that works for a variety of occasions. Doilies are glued to watering cans, collar containers, cover heart picks, and even provide a distinctive touch to a romantic bouquet of roses. A large crocheted doily repeats the motif and is tied with a sheer ribbon, swathing a tall container. Doily delightful—everything here effervesces with charm.

Paper lace & roses

Add a touch of whimsy to a bouquet of roses. Simply snip into the center of small paper doilies, wrapping them into small cones at the base of each rose, and secure the lace collar with a piece of clear tape. It's a unique look that adds *élan* to the beauty of the roses, and it's sure to appeal to the customer who's searching for something just a bit different.

victorian garden valentines

A touch of Victoria for Valentine's Day

Reminiscent of Victorian times, these feminine, keepsake boxes bring a nostalgic sense of romanticism to a Valentine display. One box lid is suspended by an elegant ribbon while an opened box presents a heart full of heather. The boxes, covered in a floral paper, evoke memories of wallpaper in old houses, and combine artfully with the garden ambiance of luscious, loosely arranged bouquets in carved stone-like urns. Fabric flowers in soft, pastel shades and fresh heather complete the garden-like appearance of the display. An unusual touch, suggestive of stone garden balusters, is the finial-shaped form covered with foliage, which tops the arrangement on the left. For the romantic at heart, the look of an old Victorian garden is the perfect valentine.

Aged planter

Create the look of an aged stone planter with this simple faux-finish paint technique. First, spray the container with soapy water followed by moss green floral spray paint; then repeat the process with soapy water and brown paint. Experiment with other shades of paint and soapy water until you get the look you want.

red, white, and clear

Red roses repeat the message

Here's a display that provides a solution for those who yen for nothing other than roses. A happy presentation for single roses, these are tubed in vials of red-dyed water. Hanging from slender strands of red ribbon, the Valentine message is as simple as one, two, three. A dry-erase board carries hand-written sentiments done with a dry-erase marker. Even the clear glass containers have been similarly decorated, using a heart stencil and coloring the heart shape with a marker, adding romantic messages, or using Valentine self-adhesive cut-outs for vase decorations. It's so simple to create, it's almost effortless.

1 Make a heart stencil out of heavy paper, and draw hearts on glass vases with a paint marker. Lip-shaped stickers also can be added.

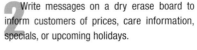

2 Write messages on a dry erase board to inform customers of prices, care information, specials, or upcoming holidays.

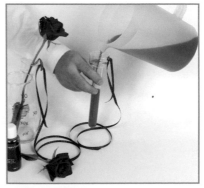

3 Add a red tint to the flower food solution of your Valentine's Day display designs with a special water color dye to increase impact.

Love's like a red, red rose

Placed side-by-side, the cut stems of *Equisetum* form a foundation which holds the single blossom at a jaunty angle. With foliage under water, be sure to use a biocide to prevent bacterial growth.

picture this

Frames and florists' foil impact rose display

Deep-hued wall frames emphasize the potted miniature roses and give them added importance by providing a contrast of deep mahogany to the pink tones of the blossoms. Small shelves provide niches to hold the terra-cotta pots of roses. Each container is decorated in a slightly different manner, using the same rose-printed wrapping paper to coordinate the trio. The top pot is left its natural color while the rim is wearing a band of glued-on decorative foil; the mid-level container is completely covered with a pot cover made of the same foil; the bottom pot's rim is left exposed, and the remainder has a shaped and glued cover made from the foil. The larger container sits on a mat, which has also been covered with matching decorative foil.

Paper valentines

Here's a solution for time-crunched Valentine's Day. Wrap a cylinder vase with decorative wrapping paper, extending the paper 4-5 inches above the vase opening. Tie a coordinating length of ribbon around the lower half of the vase, and hot-glue a heart bead on the ribbon knot. Drop in a rose so that it sits atop the paper tube.

perfect banner

Copper accessories complement peach blossoms

A banner that echoes the tones of flowers and metal, as well as the heart shape of the copper mold, ties the elements into a finished display. An exciting design of warm peach lilies, lavender *Delphinium*, and creamy snapdragons is perfectly complemented by the distinctive hue of metallic copper. A copper, heart-shaped mold is tied with raffia to the neck of the clear glass vase, which holds the premier design; a smaller, coordinating arrangement fills one of two copper baskets in the display.

1 Fold selected fabric into thirds so that unfinished edges won't show, and iron into a sharp crease.

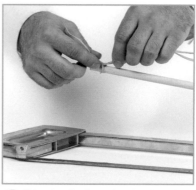

2 Cut a length of wooden dowel an inch longer than the width of the fabric banner. Tie raffia to each end of the dowel to create a hanger.

3 Fold fabric over the dowel, making sure that both ends meet at the bottom.

A dash of different

A clutch of spectacular coppery peach tulips and a few blades of variegated lily grass make an exciting alternate choice for a Valentine vase. This one clearly carries its heart inside—a small heart shaped by rolling and flattening copper beading wire, which is secured about halfway down the vase with more wire loosely placed on the container.

rising to the occasion

Christmas blooms transition into Valentine's Day

Moving from the intensely busy days of Christmas decorating into another hectic holiday can often leave you a bit empty of new ideas. A multi-level stance of permanent, intensely red amaryllis blossoms can go straight from a Christmas display to a romantic one for Valentine's Day with the addition of a twiggy heart and a heart-shaped box lid. Scarlet blossoms seem to be growing from metal urns of two different heights and from a clear glass one which allows the "roots" of the bulb to show. The box lid, utilized as a tray, is overflowing with smooth river stones, and cut grass is tucked inside one of the containers. Woody vines add movement and interest, creating a further natural touch. Backing everything are two sheets of opaque Lexan greenhouse siding, which bring light into the design, and the same material used as a mat beneath the composition creates interesting shadows that reflect the tall containers.

Different color rose

Galax "roses" are created by positioning leaves one around the other like the petals of a rose and securing them at the base with thin-gauge wire, then inserting them alongside stunning red roses—*Vive la différence*!

wallpapered magic

Softly hued papers enhance Valentine display

There are so many beautiful wallpapers available today, and it's a medium quickly turned into an appealing romantic display to complement the beauty of flowers. Choose a pastel monotone border in shades of pink and rose and a plainer design in a coordinating solid color to create an enchanting display for Valentine's Day. Construct circular pedestals and a folding screen to highlight Valentine florals arranged in clear glass vases. To shape the screen, simply score a four-foot single sheet of foam board, and cover it with the plain wallpaper and matching wallpaper border. Pedestals of different heights are made from a tall cylinder of sonotube, available from a mortar or concrete company. An inverted plastic tray forms the top. These coordinated display pieces are simple to assemble but strong on impact and clearly underscore the romance of the holiday.

Light-hearted touch

Though formal and traditional in style and placement of its individual parts, this composition, featuring snapdragons, roses, and carnations, receives a light-hearted touch with a crocheted heart picked into a crocheted doily which has been pinched at the center and wired to a wood pick.

april showers

Showers of flowers welcome spring

Bring spring to your shop with this light-hearted flower-showered umbrella and a pair of child's rain boots. Scatter odds and ends blossoms from the workroom grab box over a bright pink umbrella, and glue in place. Cut "raindrops" from clear plastic vinyl, and paint them a pastel blue or even pale lavender; the puddles beneath the umbrella and boots are created in the same way. You could also use an inexpensive plastic shower curtain in the same manner to eliminate the extra step of painting the cutouts, if you wish. Nothing quite says "spring" like April showers that bring May flowers!

1 Spray the surface of a piece of heavy duty clear plastic vinyl with water.

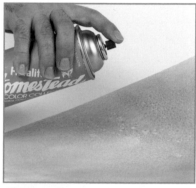

2 Follow with spray paint. Let plastic to be used for puddles dry flat and plastic for raindrops streak.

3 Cut out puddle shapes and raindrops. Add to display of umbrella and rain boots.

Fresh flower topiary

Design an unusual topiary by using a clear glass cylinder vase and fresh flowers. Glue the vase into the center of a clay pot filled with dry foam. Arrange a colorful bouquet of flowers to drop into the cylinder.

tulipmania

Oversize tulips speak of spring

Made from that ever-versatile material, foam-centered board, these giant lemon-yellow tulips are spray painted in a darker shade of yellow to delineate individual petals, and they draw the eye to twin gatherings of permanent tulips. Loose stems of buttery yellow tulips have been casually dropped into a tall market container to attract the single stem buyer while a delightful arrangement of cream tulips exploding around a sheer, yellow plaid bow and ribbon are arranged in a metal watering can to tempt the buyer who wants a finished arrangement. Nothing says spring better than tulips, one of the earliest flowers to cast winter behind. And what better way to convince customers that it's time to begin thinking of spring flower purchases to brighten their homes?

Subtle sophistication

An elegantly subtle, sophisticated color palette of soft yellow "Roma" carnations and shades of green lends distinction to these compact Biedermeier designs. Artichokes and baubles (*Berzelia*) furnish green notes to a solid design encircled by artificial river root. These baby Biedermeiers are quick to create for profitable cash-and-carry offerings, and customers may choose a single arrangement or multiples.

coordination counts!

Placement and presentation are sure to get noticed

It doesn't matter how wonderful your merchandise lines are or how varied – if they aren't coordinated in a pleasing display, the sales won't be what you hoped for. Products with similar motifs and colors work better together when coordinated and lead effortlessly into add-on sales after the customer's initial purchase. Here spring greens and white, sparked with roses, highlight the melee of coordinated ceramics and balloons. Even the ceramic picture frame carries a rose motif cut from a matching balloon to totally coordinate the display. The permanent roses dropped in ceramic vases and the vibrant pink one captured in the frame draw the eye unerringly through the display.

Vase *au naturel*

Create an unusual but distinctive container by wrapping a utility cylinder container with graceful lengths of bear grass. First cut off the heavy white ends of the grass, arrange it around the vase, then secure it with two rubber bands.

16

lamp shade topiaries

Themes bring it all together

These premade lamp shade topiaries can be created from scratch by gluing shredded moss to inverted foam shapes and forms and adding multiple stems for the trunks. A small foam ball is glued on top like a lamp finial. Similarly, creating blooming topiaries like these premade examples is easy by gluing dried rosebuds to foam shapes and "planting" them in terra-cotta pots. To complete the display—whether you choose premades or to customize each design—add themed products like this topiary birdhouse, topiary candles, and topiary-painted tabletop canvas screen.

Fragrant roses

Delight visitors to your shop by placing this mini trug of purple roses, a color that indicates that this is among the most fragrant of roses, near the cash register, so that their perfume will tempt a sniff and an additional purchase.

the name of the rose

Variety labeling aids customers

Computer generated labels for flower varieties can be easily laminated at a copy center. Cut out the laminated labels, and use spray adhesive to adhere them to glass cylinders.

Today's flower shop customer is more educated than in the past and is not always content to choose a rose by its color alone. Some may even be familiar with specific varieties, and it's quite gratifying to the customer who's seeking a specific rose to be able to find it immediately. You can make the choosing process a simple one by using tall, clear containers to showcase the different rose varieties that you carry and by providing a smart label for each container. Create identifying signs on your computer and printer, and take them to a copy center to be laminated. Attach the signage to the glass cylinders with spray adhesive at the same level on each container, so customers can easily skim the names of the varieties to find their favorites. Making the signs is easy for you to do, and it results in an extra touch of professionalism.

Sleek monofloral vase

This stark minimalist vase arrangement is the kind that is seen more and more frequently in decorating magazines. Foliage has been stripped from the roses, and the monofloral design is complemented by a single grace note— a pink craft foam heart floating inside the frosted vase at water level.

high rise display

Add a touch of whimsy to light-hearted designs

Chicken wire, permanent ivy foliage, Styrofoam™, ribbons and roses are combined to create a lofty display with a touch of whimsy. Begin by building a three-layer square Styrofoam™ base, supported by four Styrofoam™ ball "feet." The edges of all three layers of the foundation are covered with foam-centered board and then with permanent ivy leaves. Fanciful gatherings of roses and ribbon accent the piece, and the top of the chicken wire tower is formed into the shape of a perky bird.

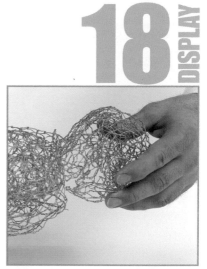

1 Shape pieces of chicken wire into balls, forming a small "head" and larger "body" ball. Wire the balls together.

2 Cut two rectangles for wings and a larger one for the tail. Fold each in half, gather cut edges and wire to the body.

Garden novelty

3 For the beak, cut two stems at an angle. Glue together, and glue to "head" ball. Wire the bird to the peak of the cage.

Garden fresh florals, arranged in groupings, appear to be growing behind a fence in this delightful wooden container fashioned of wooden pickets and decorated with a miniature garden spade and fork. The tiny tools can even be used later for terrarium gardening. It's a natural design that's a "natural" for gardeners!

FOXGLOVE
$0.00

ROSES
$0.00

HYDRANGEA
$0.00

framing your prices

Easy pricing for permanent singles

Permanent floral stems can be showcased in a market display that relegates each variety to its own tall metal container. Make it easy for your customer to choose from a full display and "gather" her own bouquet. She'll never lose sight of the price per stem and the total for her bouquet when you provide framed prices affixed to each container. Besides, she'll feel very knowledgeable, as she'll be able to name each type of flower that she chooses as she references each label. Here small photo frames have been used to serve as pricing labels. Put a white piece of paper inside the little frames as a backing, and write your price on the glass with a dry-erase marker. Prices and variety names can be easily erased, and the frames can be used again and again.

Little bunches of glory

This composition is formed of mix-and-match bunches of permanent spring flowers, *Muscari*, *Ranunculi*, daffodils, and tulips, bound in clusters with waterproof tape and inserted on a wood pick. The final effect is a grouped harmony of bunches arranged at different heights.

garden topiary

Easy-to-make topiaries for window display

Create a classic, inexpensive display that you can use for years, one that will be especially attractive to your gardening customers. Paint terra-cotta pots and trunks on white artist's canvas stretchers purchased at an art supply store, and cut plastic boxwood mats in different sizes and shapes to form the green topiary for each panel; then position each canvas panel into a carpet of the plastic boxwood. Extend the display with a scattering of clay pots.

Branch blooms

This trio of single-variety mass arrangements places snowballs (*Viburnum*), lilacs (*Syringa*), and Bridal Wreath (*Spiraea*) in lined cardboard boxes that have been covered with a plethora of *Galax* leaves applied with spray adhesive.

delightful daisy wraps

Daisy dots on cellophane make a lively display

Cut cellophane to fit each vase, and attach with tape. Cover board props for the background in the same manner.

Patterns have an innate attraction for the human personality; we love seeing patterns in our environment and our décor. This daisy motif is a lively and enduring one that appeals to our subliminal sense of joy and brings it quickly bubbling to the surface. Merchandise daisy-wrapped bunches and single stems of the perky blossom in daisy-decorated vases. The background for this intriguing exhibit is more of the daisy-printed cellophane in white, purple, or yellow daisies wrapped around rectangles of mat board in purple or white. Another section of cellophane-wrapped mat board placed beneath the display marks the boundaries of this happy vignette.

Classic spring basket

A flower-filled basket is an eternal favorite spring design, but a deeper color scheme gives this one added impact. *Anemones*, *Freesias*, tulips, and hyacinths collected in a simple woven basket foretell the approaching season with deep purple, pure white, and vibrant yellow-orange.

scentsational sales

Showcase fragrant candles and *Cosmos* for appealing display

The scent of a flower shop is unique, distinctive, and evocative of pleasant times and things. Capitalize on that unique quality with a display of scented candles, color coordinated to match permanent blossoms. Here banded candles in vibrant hues are paired with permanent *Cosmos*, which repeat the candle tints. The flowers are attached to a muslin drape and create the illusion of a spill of beautiful, fragrant flowers, enhanced by the scent of the candles. Since both candle colors and silk flowers are prone to fade when set in direct sunlight, this display is best for in-store placement. And since wonderful scents are a flower shop trademark, never be without merchandise on display that enhances it.

Clever garden pots

Use waterproof glue to fasten stems of fresh heather to terra-cotta pots. It's the perfect choice for this type of application, since it will adhere moist materials well. This garden-like design gathers *Veronica*, *Agapanthuses*, statice, *Galax* leaves, and permanent pansies and is finished off with a band of knotted raffia.

easter's on the way

Oversized display props provide impact

Dyed eggs and daffodils — traditional harbingers of Easter — make a colorful statement in this display appropriate for inside the store or in the window. Oversized eggs shaped from foam-centered board and spray painted in traditional Easter shades of rose and lilac are highlighted with sprayed-on dots and stripes, and the pot of daffodils is easy, too. Place the foam-centered board eggs and daffodil pot on a section of artificial turf or even a green shag throw rug; scatter a few pastel artificial eggs about, and your display is ready for the holiday.

1 Cut a wavy scalloped edge at the top of a yellow paper cup. Hot-glue a small square piece of foam board to the bottom of the cup to create a flat surface.

2 Draw a three-petal pattern onto yellow paper plates, extending to and incorporating the edges of the plates. Cut out the pattern.

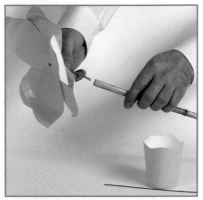

3 Pierce the center of the petals with a heavy-gauge, hairpin-shaped wire, and hot-glue the wire into a piece of bamboo to create a stem. Hot-glue the flat base of the cup to the center of the petals.

Daffodil basket

This lovely basket looks like daffodils and pussy willow have been freshly picked from the garden when, in actuality, they are permanent and dried materials.

bunny playland

Display overflows with bunnies and balloons

Gather a plethora of Easter-themed merchandise for this winsome display that features balloons, Easter bunnies, eggs, picture frames, and beverage mugs. The items can be a totally coordinated line, as we've used here, or similar items that all carry an Easter theme. Since multi-colors are used, the tints are not the most important element but rather the individual items of merchandise that contribute to the complete display. High-flying mylar balloons back the exhibit while floppy-eared bunnies peek through a white picket fence, purchased at a garden center and set into round terra-cotta saucers filled with clipped mats of boxwood. This filled-to-bursting display is sure to get your customers into an Easter-buying mood.

A little happy

This small slatted and handled basket, painted a dazzling chartreuse, is just the right contrast for the vibrant pinks, oranges, yellows, and lavenders of the cheerful profusion of *Gerberas*, *Asters*, and *Hypericum*. A defining touch is created by affixing pieces from a beaded garland to blades of bear grass and inserting them throughout the design. It makes a winsome choice for either Easter or spring.

stripe it up

Striped backdrop mimics gift bag

Creating a matching setting for coordinated merchandise gives added importance to all the items in a display. Here we've attached a sheet of yellow poster board with spray adhesive to a cut-to-size piece of foam board, then layered on ribbons vertically in hues that coordinate with the gift bag and striped Easter egg-shaped containers. The ribbons' vertical placement and different textures and widths spark interest with their opposition to the horizontal stripes of the gift bag and ceramics. The ribbon ends are lapped over to the reverse side of the foam board to hide raw edges and are snugly secured with spray adhesive. A hanger for the backdrop can be fashioned with a length of floral wire and hot glue.

1 Use spray adhesive to cover a sheet of foam-centered board with brightly colored posterboard.

2 Create stripe patterns by stretching multiple colored ribbons across the length of the foam-centered board. Fold ribbon around edge and secure each end with hot glue.

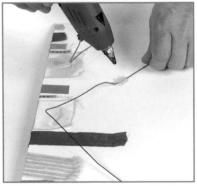

3 Add a hanger to the backside of the board by securing a piece of sturdy wire, attaching each end with hot glue.

Easter dressing

Craft foam provides an Easter dress for carnation plants. Pink craft foam is folded up and fitted around a pot for size, then stapled. Slip the potted carnation into its new cover, and tie on a length of plaid ribbon.

26

lively easter rabbit

Colorful carrots focus rabbit display and adorn container

A cartoon rabbit and picket fence cut from foam-centered board usher in the spring holiday. Assembly isn't difficult; even the carrots, made of shaped pieces of plastic foam and wrapped in orange paper ribbon, are easy to make. Preserved sprengeri fern is hot glued on to make the carrot's top. To make the bunny, first place a piece of foam-centered board against a wall; using an overhead projector, focus the rabbit image onto the board. Trace the image with a pencil. Next cut out the shape with a utility knife. Spray paint pieces in the colors shown, and use markers for eyes and nose. Outline all pieces with a black marker, using your finger to provide a guide around the edges of the piece. When paint is dry, assemble the rabbit pieces using hot glue or double-faced tape.

Carrot container

Lengthwise-sliced carrots are attached to a utility container; a row of parsley provides the carrots' tops, and everything is tied together with a wired ribbon and bow.

easter bunny

Hop into spring with the Easter bunny and oversized eggs

Create this charming Easter bunny for a delightful welcome to the season. Hot glue permanent ivy leaves to the rabbit shape, which is cut from foam-centered board, and tie a sheer ombre ribbon around his neck. Cracked "eggshells" add an original element, and "grass" is made from individual blades of dried and painted flax.

1 Inflate a latex balloon. Dip the smooth end into a mixture of plaster of paris. Repeat for a thick coating, allowing plaster to dry in between.

2 Allow to dry. Pop the balloon and break off edges to form "cracked" look.

3 Spray with pastel floral colors to create a dyed egg look.

Garden plantings

Deliciously fragrant, blue hyacinths are arranged in rimless pots that have been covered in backward-facing *Galax* leaves. Leaf stems are removed before they are attached to the pot with spray adhesive.

memo reminders

Simple materials create display statement

Like finishing a sentence with a punctuation mark, this display says, "Do it now; don't forget to say thank-you to that invaluable co-worker." A subtle reminder without signage, this message is clearly stated. Created with ordinary materials and an intriguing color combination of tan and soft yellow, no words are required. Sheets torn from a yellow steno pad and attached in a random pattern to corkboard pedestals, reminiscent of familiar office accoutrement, point the way to Administrative Professionals Day. Shaped cork panels and a roll of corkboard provide a fitting backdrop.

1 To create the corkboard panels, use a paint can lid as a pattern to cut rounded corners for a detailed look.

2 Glue cut-to-size panels to a cardboard box (different sizes of boxes if you wish) to complete the pedestals.

3 Attach steno sheets to cork backgrounds with yellow push-pins.

Penciled design

A clutch of green #2 pencils adds a touch of height to these retro office designs. Sheets of paper torn from a legal sized tablet and cut into strips are used to cover both the glass cylinder vase and the smaller clay pot.

lavender appreciation

Our display mimics gift motif with a custom banner

Whatever theme or line of merchandise you've chosen for Administrative Professionals Week, accent the motif by creating a color-coordinated backdrop to pump up the size and presence of the display. Our containers and beverage cups—always popular for this occasion—are done in mid-range lavender, and since the daisy graphic is central to the theme, we've matched it with felt cutouts on a felt banner, which is used as a backdrop for multiples of giftware and floral-balloon arrangements. Felt is a material that lends itself to cutouts, since the edges won't ravel, and the rich texture and weight of the fabric adds importance to any exhibit. Be inventive, be creative—turn practically any motif into a much larger-scaled display.

Profusion of violet

Silver and lavender say thank-you to a much-appreciated assistant in the most elegant of ways. This arrangement brings its message in multiple shades of lavender, as the enticing scent and texture of purple spring hyacinths burst aloft from sprays of statice.

just bag it

A plethora of brown bags creates a showcase

A collection of cord-handled, brown bags was chosen to make a stylish yet quick-to-construct display appropriate for a shop window. It would also work especially well inside the store to draw a customer's eyes to gift bags and permanent florals displays. All that's needed is sixteen small bags and three matching, larger ones plus a piece of foam-centered board. Attach the small ones, equally spaced as shown, to the foam-centered board. Then randomly fill some, but not all, of the little bags with poufs of yellow tissue paper and a variety of permanent blossoms. We chose a mixture of pink *Dahlias* and poppies and a touch of lavender freesia to contrast with the neutral beige of the bags.

1 Glue the back panel of each small bag to the foam-centered board, spacing the bags evenly.

2 Place petite bunches of permanent flowers in a few of the bags.

3 Pinch the center of sheets of tissue paper, fluff the edges and insert into bags.

Divine structure

Love the look of a structured design? Spray the inside of a disposable plant saucer with leaf shine; then place a thin layer of clipped bear grass in the saucer and spray with adhesive. Repeat this process several times. Then set the structure atop a pot and insert a few English roses.

31

flowers for mom

Humorous display for Mother's Day

Reminding us all of childhood efforts to present Mom with flowers, this white picket fence brings a comical touch to those memories, as we note the empty stems among the other blossoms "growing" against a white picket fence. Sure to elicit a smile with its cartoon-like air, this display appeals to emotions that are at the seat of every sale. The flowers are actually inserted into foam beneath the seamless green paper, which serves as a manicured "lawn." Themed displays like this one create interest and attract viewers to pause for just a moment for a closer look; after that first response, they tend to react on an emotional level, relating the display in some way to their own experiences. Just as this particular display is geared toward buying flowers for Mom, planning differently themed displays throughout the year can generate profitable sales year round.

Gerberas highlighted

A simple design begins with pushing stems of Lily grass (*Liriope*) into glass beakers and allowing the flexible grass to curl around the inside of the bulbous bottom of the vase, creating a swirling effect. The various heights of foliage which extend from the vase opening accentuate the placement of a single *Gerbera* and double the impact of a lone blossom, creating an inexpensive cash-and-carry sale.

ribbon rug

Snippets of ribbon create depth and texture

Get lots of mileage from this easy technique. Add an impressive dollop of color by constructing a backdrop made from bits of ribbon cut from several color-coordinated spools in solids, stripes, plaids, or other patterns. Cut short sections of ribbons from the different spools, scrunch the pieces together, and glue them to a large section of foam-centered board. Fill out the display with an assortment of color-coordinated hatboxes. We accented our display of saturated blues with a splash of intense pink permanent *Dahlias*, lime green *Viburnums* and a green lady slipper orchid plant—all captured in tall squared ceramic containers.

1 To construct the beribboned backdrop, cut several 2-3-inch lengths of ribbon from different but color-coordinated spools.

2 Scrunch the pieces of wired ribbon in your hands to create a crimped effect.

3 Glue crimped ribbon snips in a random fashion to a piece of foam-centered board.

Lime ice and popsicle pink

The intense shades of color in this design literally make it pop. Lime *Viburnums*, hot pink *Ranunculi*, and sweet peas in an airy, delicately old-fashioned bouquet belie its thoroughly contemporary color scheme.

beautifully bordered

Textured borders create a pleasing presentation

For a delightfully decorative look, cover foam-centered board frames and a variety of glass or metal containers with textured vinyl borders. These heavily textured white borders are available at wallpaper and home improvement stores and lend themselves to an array of uses. To achieve the muted pink cast shown here, spray floral paint onto a damp sponge, and rub it onto the border to emphasize the raised design. To achieve the professionally mitered look at the corners of the picture frames, simply overlap the ends of the borders, then score them at a 45-degree angle with an artist's knife. The final result resembles vintage pressed tin, which is enjoying a resurgence in popularity for decorative accents. And the borders provide an easy way to create a variety of matching elements to exhibit in your window. Here permanent old-fashioned garden roses are used to create a lovely display for Mother's Day.

Spray floral paint onto a damp sponge, and rub it onto the vinyl border for an enhanced raised effect.

Antique papers

Resembling "Shabby Chic" style, this metal pail is covered with a vintage-look floral paper. The paper's rose motif is continued with the creamy yellow roses in the bouquet and with the mauve and deep pink of the flowering kale and *Hydrangea*.

pink persuasion

Vibrant pink entices a second look

Sheets of craft foam are the key ingredient to a fetching Mother's Day display. We've used printed images from a floral calendar to highlight our holiday ensemble. A favorite shade of pink creates an air of femininity, and, of course, pastel pink permanent roses combined with other pink blossoms sketch a world of possibilities for Mother's Day giving. The edges of the calendar pages have been trimmed away, and they are mounted on rectangles of matching craft foam.

1 Trim edges of a page from a calendar to desired size.

2 Use spray adhesive to attach the calendar image to craft foam.

3 Cut a section of craft foam to fit around a glass cylinder vase and glue in place.

Sweet boxes

Small-scaled compositions of roses, Canterbury bells (*Campanula*), *Cyclamen* blossoms, and *Cymbidium* orchids are sure to please the most discerning mother. The wooden boxes are painted a delicate shade of pink and finished with a silvered scallop shell.

chapeaus for mom

Flowers accent straw hats for Mom—on her special day

For Mother's Day, feature fanciful topiaries showcasing a collection of beautifully decorated hats sure to catch the eye of the customer seeking an unusual gift for Mom. Straw hats in varying styles are embellished with lush permanent roses and exquisite ribbons—elegant enough to wear to church or for the stylish gardener! The unusual topiaries not only provide display props but are salable as additional gift ideas. Glue dry foam into inexpensive clay pots that have been spray painted gold. Insert a gold-painted plastic extender rod into the foam. Cover the foam with pebbles or moss, and spray with the gold paint. Glue the foam spheres to the top of the extender rod. Attach coordinating blossoms or moss to the spheres.

Hat with fresh flowers

There's nothing quite so lovely as fresh flowers, and how unexpected to find them these days adorning a hat. Glue a few fresh asters to a casual hat tied with contrasting ribbon, and suggest it to your regular customers for themselves or for Mom to wear for a special occasion.

just hangin' around

Ribboned baskets create drop display

A collection of beautifully coordinated baskets gains extra importance when displayed at different levels. Two baskets of varying sizes hang suspended from lavender ribbons while three larger ones are arranged beneath on a flat surface. The largest basket of the nested group and two coordinated decorative boxes rest on the tabletop, showing the containers' painted rose décor to the greatest advantage. The basket at eye level carries a design of permanent roses in two sizes and shades, with a twig bird's nest nestled in the center, delightfully repeating the rosy theme and accomplishing the goal of creating a display that showcases a consistent motif in different shapes and sizes.

Jewel affection

A novel boxed arrangement is created by filling a white heart-shaped plastic box with waxflowers and silver sage (*Salvia*). A half-inch thick layer of floral foam lines the box, and pieces of waxflowers are inserted vertically. Stems of silver sage are inserted around the edge, and a twirl of sheer ribbon completes a jewel-box presentation.

indoor gardens

Wire fencing and clay pots bring the outdoors in

For the mother who gardens, or anyone who loves the look of outdoor plants inside, this display gets customers thinking about cultivating and planting in a renewal of season. Wire fencing provides airy, sturdy pedestals for clay pots holding permanent artichokes and lilies. The pedestal in the background is based in a large clay saucer, and the cylinder itself is filled with smaller pots randomly stacked. The pedestal in the foreground not only holds a pot of lilies but encircles another pot filled with "bulbs" just beginning to break into foliage.

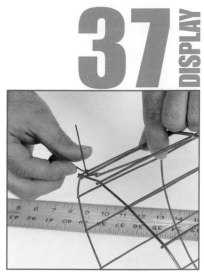

1 Cut a 34-inch wide piece of farm fence to fit the circumference of an 11-inch round tray. Wire ends of fence together to form a cylinder shape.

2 Place wire column into a clay container and randomly stack smaller clay pots inside.

3 Place an upside down, 11-inch round tray on the top of the wire pedestal.

The art of spring

It's almost like a sculpture, yet this tall arrangement betrays its gardeny roots with a burst of fiery color. The permanent parrot tulips in this design enliven drab days and forecast invigorating days ahead.

 38 accentuate your bouquets

Show bouquets to best advantage with silken banners

Emphasize a shop window display of bouquets with elegant, wide ribbon banners that highlight design style and provide importance to smaller-scaled arrangements. Although bouquets are often labor-intensive and costly, they may be the most challenging to display effectively, but panels of color made from 12-inch-wide wired ribbon draw instant attention to these bouquets made of permanent flowers. The ribbon is hung like draped fabric; if the wired edges prevent the lengths of ribbon from flowing smoothly, clip the wire and remove it. An additional section of ribbon is gathered and tied into a large bow to complete the line of the colorful ribbon banners.

Charmed flowers

For an appealing, affordable arrangement of pastel roses and miniature carnations, a wash of gold paint and a brass "bow" charm provide a unique touch to a humble terra-cotta container. Charms in a variety of shapes and sizes are available at craft stores and add personality to everyday containers. Accessorizing small arrangements with craft charms gives added value.

39

faux bridal cakes

Frosted foam bases make realistic confections

An attractive enticement, these realistic-looking cakes designed for display can attract brides-to-be into your shop. Both cakes are created by frosting layers of plastic foam (they can be reused many times with different permanent floral designs). And more—they are easily transported for use in bridal show booths or placed in your wedding consultation area as a permanent reference for selling cake flowers. The round cake shown is built with plastic revere bowls used as risers for each layer, and the topmost bowl displays a gathering of posies. Two-toned lengths of ribbon band the bottom of each "cake" layer and coordinate with the permanent flowers used at both the top and bottom of the ensemble. Consult your local baker about making display cakes, and be sure to ask that each layer be separately iced, to allow for different configurations.

Design whimsy

This one's quick to assemble and makes great use of short-stemmed or broken-stem flowers. Saturate a floral foam sphere with flower-food solution, and arrange blossoms into the sphere, making sure that the foam doesn't show. Then set the whimsical "ball" into a contemporary vase.

sphere music

Unique designs utilize foam-centered board

Interlocking armillary spheres pierced by arrows are fashioned from foam-centered board to build a unique display that can be tailored to different uses. Set atop foam-centered-board boxes, which have been covered in moss and highlighted with permanent *Hydrangeas* in soft shades of green and white, this unusual creation is suitable for a casual outdoor garden gathering as a sundial centerpiece or as a rental piece, where its mystic interlocking spheres symbolize the unity of marriage. The display's resemblance to garden ornamentation makes it wonderful for garden weddings.

1 Cut three concentric rings from a piece of black foam-centered board. Cut three strips of foam board, each the length of the circumference of one ring. Hot-glue the strips onto the edges of the corresponding ring.

2 In the outside bands of each of the two smallest rings, cut two notches opposite each other that are the thickness of the foam board. Slip the smallest ring inside the middle-sized ring, then the middle-sized ring inside the largest ring.

Miniature garden

Reminiscent of Victorian times, this miniature greenhouse, or terrarium, brings the delight of a garden indoors. Planted with two varieties of fern, a small *Begonia*, and a miniature rose, it brings inside the earthy scent of the forest floor.

3 Add an aged spatter finish with gold spray paint by slightly depressing the spray nozzle. Make an arrow from foam board, and paint to match. Place the sphere atop another dowel rising from a decorative container.

bridal attractions

Uncomplicated new ways with wedding display

When you need an attractive wedding display, but you don't want the usual mannequin and bridal gown, here's an alternative. A collection of vintage black-and-white bridal photos in silver frames coupled with pastel-hued permanent flowers in contemporary aluminum planters captures wedding ambiance in a very personal manner. Or this cool, elegant display can be turned into a totally different, upbeat, and thoroughly modern display by using brass frames instead of silver and brightly hued blossoms instead of pastel ones. Remember, if you have a large window to fill, photos can be blown up to poster size at photo shops.

Dainty baby's breath

The popularity of baby's breath keeps it always in fashion, and it is so versatile that it can be used in many ways to grace wedding designs. Here a half bunch of this delicate blossom is banded together and placed in a foam-filled clay pot. The stems of the flowers form a natural "trunk", which is braided with ribbons matching the wedding colors.

out of africa

Dramatic design captures the spirit of adventure

Spray back of palm leaves with adhesive in an overlapping manner to cover green fabric to create a backdrop for this display.

A sparseness of materials gives this intriguing design a hint of Africa, calling to mind dense jungles and primitive spaces. Two stems of *Oncidium* orchids are divided to get the most impact yet contain costs. A bloom from a palm plant repeats the yellow of the orchids while Chinese evergreen foliage and *Galax* leaves echo the mystery of the jungle and create a base for towering stems. Whitewashed pods accent the bubble bowl container, which has been covered with palm leaves and set upon a carved wooden pedestal. A dark background made from palm leaves and camouflage fabric enhance the ambience of an African safari while a metal canteen, leopard-banded hat, and an oil lamp accessorize the scene and complete the feeling of the travails of travel on the dark continent—one can almost hear the roar of lions in the night.

Primeval canopy

Australia's rare fine-leafed umbrella fern (*Sticherus*) shapes a canopy above a clustered gathering of exotic blossoms: pincushions (*Leucospermum*), *Banksias*, and *Leucadendrons*. Everything is arranged in a stately rectangular basket, which rests upon its own wooden base.

exotic bamboo

River cane creates a fashionable backdrop

Bamboo never seems to go out of fashion, and its textured structure lends itself to many styles of décor. River cane mimics the look of bamboo, and here dyed river cane works well as an attractive covering for a cylindrical vase filled with that exotic favorite—orchids. These permanent orchids are displayed in front of a handcrafted screen. However, if you're pressed for time, you can purchase an inexpensive bamboo shade at a home improvement store.

1 To create the bamboo-covered container, place two rubber bands around a cylinder vase and position the bamboo under the rubber bands.

2 Tie floral wire around the bamboo in two places to permanently secure the bamboo to the vase and remove rubber bands.

3 Create the backdrop by wiring pieces of bamboo together with paddle wire near both edges of each piece. Add one piece at a time.

Dried décor accents

Pliable materials provide eye-catching convolutions in clear glass containers as they are pushed into swirls and interwoven patterns to create the illusion of motion.

44

balloons & butterflies

Fluttering butterflies and balloons light up the scene

A key component to remember when displaying coordinated merchandise is to show the customer ways of using the mugs, vases, and frames that are arranged in a display. For example, arrange mugs in an idealized serving tray constructed of pebbles that fill a painted terra-cotta saucer. Perk up a matching frame with colorful paper in place of a photograph. Get the picture? In our display, everything is keyed to the butterfly theme of the ceramics and chosen to accent the yellow and orange shades. Fresh yellow blossoms are tucked inside clear glass cylinder vases, and a bevy of faux orange butterflies add light-hearted movement to branches arranged in another vase. Crumpled bits of orange craft paper in strategic spots repeat the vivid, dominant hue of the butterflies.

Woodsy illusion

Add a woodsy note to a collection of roses in an analogous combination of pale apricot, peach, and red-orange by placing them in a moss-covered vase. A "handle" created from permanent wire vines completes the illusion of a basket gathering of blooms.

summer sizzlers

Butterfly colors grab attention

Capturing your customer's attention is easy when you showcase these colors that almost seem to pulse with the beat of a butterfly's wings. Brilliant, intensely hued plastic vases are laid horizontally side by side and stacked vertically to achieve this animated construction. Perfectly poised on the left is an arrangement of fresh asters in counter-balancing shades of purple and pink, and on the right at the bottom is a scaled-down design of smaller butterflies. And there's even a bright green ball candle that teases for candle purchases. Mid-size butterflies in monarch tints carry the mid-level of the display while the largest butterflies in soft yellow seem to be leading the viewer into more surprises.

Gazing bowl

Turn a rose bowl into a gazing ball with this upbeat design. Crisscross blades of bear grass in the bottom of the bowl to hold the orchid blossoms above the water line, then continue to layer more bear grass with different colors of blossoms. So simple and so lovely!

garden gifts

Gifts of love from the garden

Nothing expresses love quite as well as a gift from the garden; it always seems to be a gift straight from the heart. Since gardening is a hobby shared by so many, garden gifts are appropriate for many occasions — from birthdays to Mother's Day. This is a display that incorporates many elements that are natural to the garden; a tall, single-blossomed lily in a clay pot, a gathering of spectacular yellow roses in a tinted clay pot, and a foliage topiary with a braided trunk. Everything in the display is set on rough planking, with scattered sand to highlight that "just-brought-in-from-the-garden" look. A shadow box of gloriously colored butterflies and votive candles in brightly-hued petite pots make this a striking display that retains that fresh yet stunningly beautiful look that only comes from a garden.

Flower baskets

An assortment of handled baskets in different sizes are hung from ribbon streamers — these are perfect for May Day gifts or for Mother's Day displays. Affordably priced and filled with daisies and carnations in a monochromatic color choice, they look as if they've been snipped from the garden.

clay pot mania

Terra-cotta pots make a clever presentation

Yearning for an escape from our stressful lives and returning to a quieter lifestyle has made gardening a great pastime and clay pots a great decorating item of the decade. This display showcases many ways to utilize all sizes of pots. Glass cylinders are filled with miniature pots and pot shards, more shards fill a glass dome, and there's even a clever topiary formed of tiny pots glued to a plastic foam sphere. Create the display for pennies, and watch your profits soar.

1. Hot-glue miniature clay pots onto a four-inch-diameter plastic foam ball, with the bottom ends of the pots against the ball.

2. Leave space to hot-glue one two-inch-diameter clay pot to the ball; this will be the bottom of the ball. Fill in spaces between the pots with moss.

3. Fill a six-inch-diameter pot with dry foam. Then hot-glue a two-inch-diameter pot upside down into the foam, and stack other same-sized pots on top of it to create the stem.

Garden inspired topiary

Small clay pots are glued together and impaled on a wooden dowel, which is anchored in foam glued into the larger pot. The top pot has a liner and moist foam to hold a collection of garden flowers.

garden vegetables

Indoor garden designs of vegetables and flowers

Highlight permanent vegetables with vegetable motif fabric and matching vegetable design ribbon in this remarkable display. Create a one-of-a-kind whimsical topiary with fabric cut and glued to a foam-board shape. The topiary is given added dimension by flat, layered surfaces and is glued to a sturdy branch of curly willow planted in a clay pot. More of the fabric is glued to a cardboard tube, which is encircled with wire fencing. A wire basket holds more vegetables to complete the theme of a prolific vegetable garden. It's an inspiring garden display for warm summer days and showcases elements that would bring added touches to a home kitchen.

Basket garden

Bring the garden indoors with this basket, alive with lilies, potted *Gerberas*, stonecrop, and a vivid swirl of lively tulips at the basket's edges. Burlap ribbon and lichen-covered spheres incorporate texture into this vivacious design.

49

birds, bugs, and butterflies

A touch of the garden for indoors, patio, or porch

For outdoor living, or to bring the garden look inside, these delightfully decorated houses are the perfect accent. Both the bluebird house and the butterfly house sport roofs charmingly shingled with dried flowers. A shadow box, which displays the same blossoms hot-glued in place, and the whimsical "bug" display almost create an instant garden. The tiny arrangement of bird, bird's nest, and fresh spray roses in a small terra-cotta pot gives it all a finishing touch. The antiqued surface on which the vignette sits provides country store charm. Paved with wood boards that have been wiped with a sponge soaked in diluted acrylic paint, the base is easy to make for both tabletops or display window floors.

Plate of flowers

Attention-grabbing, this plate full of posies is an unusual presentation of a collection of dried blossoms, which have been hot-glued to a ceramic plate. Be sure to place similarly decorated plates in more traditional settings—hung on a wall or displayed on a decorative easel —to show your customer ways to exhibit it in her own home.

50

go balloonistic with flowers!

Display daisies for low-budget fun

Simple balloon flowers on foam-centered board stems provide "daisy power"—wherever they're placed, they provide a bright spot of cheer. Fashion them by first tying stems of two underinflated nine-inch diameter white latex balloons together, making two pairs; then tie the two pairs together to create the four-petaled flower. Next, tie a five-inch diameter yellow balloon into the center of the white cluster, and attach the completed balloon daisy to a stem, which has been cut from foam-centered board and covered with green satin ribbon. Plant these daisy flowers in clay pots, and use them on tables, or create a happy entranceway to your shop by placing them on both sides of a decorative path.

Party-time centerpiece

Coordinating with the large balloon daisies, this imaginative table piece utilizes both balloons and fresh blossoms. Butter yellow button spray mums are arranged at varying levels in a four-inch diameter white clay pot to form the center of the "daisy," then six underinflated nine-inch diameter white latex balloons are wired to wooden picks and arranged around the rim of the pot to make the petals. Ribbon completes the tabletop design that can inspire party sales from your shop's daisy motif.

connect the dots

Extend patterns for a coordinated look

Coordinated products demand matched settings to enhance sales, and unique offerings such as these dotted containers lend themselves to incomparable display ideas. Even the dotty boxes in which the vases were packaged are utilized as risers in this vignette. Craft foam in a turquoise that exactly matches the merchandise is dotted with round yellow labels to extend the theme throughout. One section hangs behind the exhibit on the wall, and another forms a base to contain the pieces. Craft foam comes in a wide range of colors, so if you have an unusual shade to match, consider using these inexpensive sheets.

1 Adhere round labeling stickers at equal increments onto a sheet of craft foam.

2 Place additional stickers in an even but staggered manner between each row.

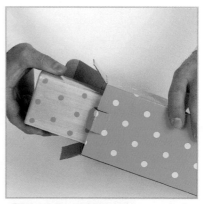

3 Unpack the products, and incorporate the coordinating boxes into the display.

Simple sophistication

A two-tiered arrangement is topped with plumes of goldenrod (*Solidago*) while a second tier shaped of radiant yellow roses, lilies, and button spray mums fills a pot that was painted with inexpensive acrylic craft paint.

oriental porcelain

Oriental ware in serene blues expresses refined elegance

Soothing, monochromatic blues are showcased in planters, ginger jars, and other porcelain pieces. The display shows cool blue to great advantage, and it's a wonderful way to provide visual relief during hot summer months. Permanent delphiniums top the display, and draw the eye for added impact while the table top is merchandised with a summer potpourri. The nested tables placed on top of the larger display surface allows for two levels on which the products can be merchandised. Antique books, boxes, and the detailing of the nested tables reinforce the traditional appeal of delftware and the color blue.

Vase collections

Individual Skyline roses are delicately surrounded by *Solidago* and inserted into coordinating delftware vases of different shapes to create a coordinated look.

blue jeans cacti

New twist for dungaree fabric and sunflowers

Sunlight streaming through a display window can quickly fade product, but here's a display that will only get better with fading. Old jeans become more like old friends as the color softens, and these unusual cacti will get better with fading, too! Shape cut-up old jeans around foamboard cutouts of cactus shapes, put fresh sunflowers into water tubes, and tuck into the jeans pockets with red bandannas. Insert nails through the fabric to simulate cactus spines. Set live cactus plants around the display cactus—they'll love a sunny window—and you're all set for summer sales. For a low maintenance display, substitute permanent sunflowers for the fresh ones.

1 Draw and cut several different cactus shapes from half-inch thick foam-centered board.

2 Cover with old jeans that have been dipped in clear wallpaper paste.

3 Pierce with nails or pieces of heavy gauge wire for spines. Add fresh or permanent florals.

"S" is for sunflowers

Sunflowers' cheery faces are difficult to pass by—everyone wants to take home an armload. Encourage that yen with a sunny clutch of this casual flower in a sisal-wrapped container.

54

cottage country

Friendly cows and colorful drieds make approachable displays

An irrepressible theme in decorating is the many faces of country, and here's a simple way to bring the homey touch of dried materials to the country "look." A hand-painted terra-cotta pot holds a fanciful arrangement of dried blossoms and foliages while the flat saucer repeats the same blossoms and pods with the look of potpourri. A raffia-banded shock of wheat leaves the impression that it's been gathered from a field just outside the door, and the single stem of dogwood planted off center in another pot simulates a naturally grown tree. Finish the display with jars of preserved jellies or fruits and a bit of primitive art showcasing that popular collectible icon of country — the Holstein cow.

Topiary treasure

A distinctive topiary is created here with an ordinary terra-cotta pot and saucer and a moss-covered sphere punctuated with glued-on dried pansies. Tied up with raffia and a smart bow on top, this "treasure" will be at home on any tabletop.

cubist art

Squares, rectangles, and cubes of brilliant color grab attention

Color-blocking makes a message emphatic and bold. And when it's used in fashion and art, it is never ignored. It's a technique that makes a smooth transfer to a florist's display and can even be used inside your cooler. Since the background blocks and rectangles (made from foam-centered board or sturdy cardboard) are wrapped with bright shades of Plastifoil®, a laminated foil, it's waterproof and impervious to cooler moisture. Choose complementary shades for the flowers you intend to use, and insert single blossoms into Blossom Boxes™, which are then hung from the decorated boards in a pleasing cubist pattern.

1 Choose colors of Plastifoil® to coordinate with the flowers used in the display.

2 Cut foam-centered board into squares and rectangles, and cover one side with foil and secure with tape.

3 Fill flower tubes with water, add flowers, and place them in the Blossom Boxes™.

Pow power

Gerberas in intense shades of red and orange cap evenly sheared stems of bear grass and cable ties, which line the sides of a clear glass vase.

56

country living

Canning jars and country flowers

The homespun theme of this gathering of dried, fresh, and permanent materials creates a setting that reflects the peaceful air of country living. Glass jars set at the base of a rustic twig chair are filled with cut-from-the-yard branches and permanent flowers. Other jars hold permanent berries "preserved" in acrylic "water," and a galvanized watering can adds a touch of simple close-to-the-earth living. A magnificent pieced quilt brings a fiery dash of color to an otherwise quiet setting, and although this setting says "country" in every detail, an old wagon wheel or other memento of bygone days could be used instead of the chair to create a quaint setting.

Countrified sheaves

The texture of country and the beauty of a spring garden are captured in these unique sheaf designs encased in glass vases, which allow millet heads to drape gracefully over the rim. Roses, *Allium*, and sunflower centers are arranged in saturated straight-handle bouquet holders and are positioned in the centers of the millet sheaves to complete the designs.

fourth of July

Patriotic red, white, and blue for firecracker day

Reminiscent of parade bunting and vintage flags, this easy-to-make backdrop signals Independence Day celebrations. The all-American look is accented with a floral design in bold red, white and blue flowers. Or, you might dress your shop window with a picnic basket overflowing with permanent flowers in traditional patriotic colors, and scatter plastic tableware in matching hues over a checked tablecloth to create a vibrant display just in time for the festive summer holiday.

1 Use a roller brush to paint "flag" stripes onto a large piece of cotton fabric.

2 Cut stars from cardboard to use as a stencil. Use the star patterns to stencil in star shapes when painting the blue section.

3 Use an almost dry roller with both blue and red paint to randomly blend the colors together. Finish by burning the edges.

Firecracker day flowers

A lively collection of hot-hued summer flowers in a clear glass container, tied off with a swath of blue ribbon and accented with a holiday badge, makes a patriotic statement.

summer fireworks

Plastic tableware and *Anthuriums* conjure a fiery show

Summer time is picnic time, and as July 4th nears, thoughts turn to a celebratory family picnic to share the fireworks. This display, done in firecracker red, sets off fireworks of its own with an unusual mosaic created from plastic tableware, matching paper napkins and summer flip flops. And not to be out-done, *Anthuriums* in their own particular shade of blazing red fill plastic drink cups and a red flower bucket. With the addition of strategically placed white, self-adhesive labels, the bucket mimics a neighboring polka-dotted ceramic pot.

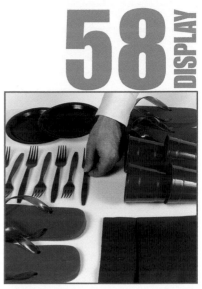

1 Lay out picnic accessories in a rectangular shape on a large piece of foam-centered board.

2 Once the pattern pleases you, glue everything in place on the foam board.

3 Attach white, circular self-adhesive pricing labels to the painted flower bucket in a polka dot pattern.

Picnic sparklers

Plant small blooming *Anthurium* plants in red plastic beverage cups to make casual centerpieces, and cover the soil surface with white aquarium gravel. Insert a matching plastic fork handle down in the pot to create a whimsical card holder which can be used for displaying the plant's price in your shop, and after purchase hold an enclosure card.

basket gatherings

A tisket, a tasket, gather it all in beautiful baskets

Nothing fits quite as easily into any kind of setting as a beautiful basket, either decorated or filled with lovely flowers. Show the many applications of baskets with this wonderful, vibrant display firmly anchored to an unfinished shelving unit available at most craft or hobby stores. Autumn-hued product decorates the baskets in different ways —the topmost basket looks as if it's just been brought in from the garden with its horizontal placement of flowers. The midpoint basket of the display is a wall piece with cascading blossoms. Other baskets sport decorated handles and are filled with freeze-dried fruit accents.

Autumn-hued tapers

Taper candles, side by side, showcase mellow fall shades of orange, yellow, sage, olive, and tan. Arranged in trays or baskets, the striped pattern draws attention to an otherwise standard offering.

nesting season

Birds' nests nurture a tranquil environment

Birds' nests, enduring icons of nature and renewal most often reminiscent of spring, provide an element of peaceful serenity in home décor at almost any season of the year but are ideal for autumn. Compotes and coordinating candlesticks, antiqued in white "cottage" style, are a striking contrast to the darker nests and floral arrangement, which is composed of dried and preserved leaves, artichokes, lichens, and grasses. The nests are cozily filled with speckled plastic eggs and add balancing texture as well as anchoring weight to the soaring vertical lines of earthen-tinted foliage and the taper candle.

Nature's icon

A simple bird's nest, shaped from nito vine, is given importance by placing it upon a circular, gray, sculpted-look platform similar to those designed to hold pillar candles. The natural look is increased by adhesive-coated bits of raffia and blades of bear grass woven loosely into the nest. A tiny feather or two gives the impression that Mother Bird will return to her home momentarily.

closet collectible

Shoe rack displays dried materials

It's an ordinary, inexpensive shoe rack that you can find at your local discount store, and it works very well indeed as an organizer for your shop's collection of dried materials—bundled and artfully displayed. Since it's an expandable fixture, it can be adjusted to hold as many varieties of preserved materials as you carry. Or, for more impact, each level can be filled with a single type of product to create a more definitive, massive look. Hanging a large swag above the rack made from the displayed materials sparks customers' own creativity and shows them how dried and preserved materials can be utilized to create something wonderful for their own homes.

Vertical expression

Unabashedly natural in appearance, this design incorporates tall grasses, including male bell grass and plume reed in both beige and chartreuse. Preserved natural green papyrus and a band of vertically arranged ocher colored leaves encircles the design and camouflages the stems of the grasses.

falling leaves

Super-size fall with huge leaves

When displays are collections of small-scale merchandise, draw attention to them with an over-sized repetition of the prevailing motif. Here giant oak leaves, which have been cut from foam-centered board, are painted with a multi-layer paint daubing technique done with crumpled paper, plastic, or cellophane. The leaves are suspended with clear monofilament and repeat the autumn leaf theme of the boxes and pots and reflect the fiery tints of the potted croton.

1 Draw various sizes of oak leaves on a piece of foam-centered board, and cut them out with an artist's or utility knife.

2 Spray paint onto a crumpled piece of cellophane, and dab paint onto each leaf, one color at a time, until the desired effect is achieved.

3 Add vein-shaped indentations onto each leaf by pressing the blunt end of a permanent marker into the foam board; color the depressions with the marker.

Tropical harvest

A gardeny mix of safflowers *(Carthamus)*, butterfly weed *(Asclepias)*, and black-eyed Susan *(Rudbeckia)* blossoms takes an exotic turn with the addition of yellow kangaroo paws *(Angiozanthos)* and broad croton *(Codiaeum)* leaves, which are used to cover the low-cost papier-mâché pot.

texture towers

Clear glass cylinders and natural materials create impact

Natural materials constrained by clear glass cylinders of varying heights lend verve to this contemporary display, which brings nature into the confines of sleek modernity. The varying sizes, shapes, colors, and textures attract the eye when the cylinders are used alone, or the collection is weighty enough to act as a backdrop for another display such as small tabletop plants or even an assemblage of gourmet products. *Equisetum*, bamboo, gravel, croton leaves, artichokes, miniature clay pots, and various kinds of pods and cones fill these containers, but other materials will work equally well.

Sphere basket

A rustic rectangular basket holds an assortment of orbs and textured materials that beg to be touched. An intriguing textural composition formed of spheres of woven vine, moss and lichen-covered orbs, and laranja pods is accented with rice flower, estrela pods, twisted ting ting, and seeded *Eucalyptus*.

ladder it

Step ladder serves as display fixture

Pressed into service as display furniture, this utilitarian stepladder has been painted white and provides shelving for varied displays from potted plants to gift ceramics. It isn't seasonally defined, so it provides an appropriate backdrop for practically every display occasion, and it can be folded and put away, requiring little in the way of storage space. Our ladder holds a pair of ceramics decorated with grapes, a motif repeated in the bowl of permanent grapes on the ladder's bottom step. The permanent kale echoes the purple tint of the grapes and ties the display to its purple and green color harmony.

Country brights

A burst of brilliant reds defines this impressive wreath, which is created of permanent *Zinnias*, roses, dried *Celosia*, preserved oak leaves, and artificial pomegranates and crab apples. The crab apples are actually a separate garland, created by wrapping copper beading wire around the stems of crab apples, spaced 5-7 inches apart. The garland is then loosely wrapped onto the wreath.

gold country

Country cupboard blends pastoral elements in a setting that feels like home

The quiet simplicity of country living is exemplified traditionally with rustic pine furnishings and warm amber tones. A cupboard and a custom-painted flea-market table in the same mellow tones warm a display that is dramatically punctuated by blue Delftware housed on the cupboard's shelves. A decorative tin ceiling tile, bucolic framed art, and a swath of plaid fabric across the tabletop create the desired ambience while faux fruits emphasize the country scene. Stems of Chinese lantern (*Sandersonia*), fresh yarrow, and roses in a glowing shade of golden yellow add the necessary floral touches to complete this tempting display.

Countrified topiary

A "tree" composed of Jonathan apples and red dogwood is a simple topiary that looks as if it belongs in a rural setting. The dogwood branches are set into floral foam inside the container and serve as picks to secure the apples. Permanent vine twined around the apples and the dogwood tree "trunk" add movement to this design, which is shaped from natural materials.

bountiful baskets

Intense chrysanthemum colors herald autumn

Inexpensive bushel market baskets, filled with a bevy of chrysanthemums in closely attuned fall shades of gold, orange, and russet, are displayed in stair-stepped style. Use this display to merchandise bunches or single stems; either way it's a quickly assembled grouping of fresh autumn flowers that is especially appropriate for fall festival promotions. When it's too cool in your area for outdoor displays, this one can be moved indoors. Bales of hay, corn shocks, pumpkins, and seasonal gourds can be added as each becomes available to stretch the fall marketing season from September right through November, as autumn matures into its full blaze of colors.

Potted autumn

Melding tones of the rust-colored pot and the 'Orange Viking' button mums, this delightfully mounded arrangement is accented with seeded *Eucalyptus* and is the perfect size to bring a bit of the harvest season indoors. Sized right for gift-giving or the kitchen counter, this one is sure to attract impulse buyers.

fall
kraft

Fall fascination expressed in drieds and colorful gourds

Show off a collection of dried botanicals in like-colored boxes, bags, and containers. Texture plays an important part in this subtle fall display of pods, papier-mâché pumpkins, and dried materials, but the unifying element is the color—shades of paper-bag brown. It's an easy-to-assemble display that doesn't require a great deal of time to construct, and it offers materials that can be used in many ways for seasonal décor. The look is earthy yet sophisticated and lends itself to the creation of arrangements or other designs incorporating the textural materials displayed. For a monochromatic backdrop, use brown kraft paper that comes in large rolls for an easy-to-make backdrop.

Gourds and garlands

A gathering of colorful gourds and fall berries displayed against torn strips of brown kraft paper highlights warm fall shades of orange and yellow. A unique garland, strung on copper wire, is made of sunflower blossoms, oak leaves, and sections of stems—materials that will all dry naturally.

spice is nice

Simple materials inspire a mosaic assemblage

Create a warm, earthy-toned display with matte board and everyday spices. Start with tan cardboard, and glue bits of dried spices in mosaic-like patterns to form attractive floral designs. The large sunflower image consists of cloves for the center, whole nutmegs for the next two rows, and bay leaves to shape the outside petals of the blossom. Additional bay leaves are added to a length of stem to create an unusually pleasing sunflower. The left grouping of flowers is done with rose hips and cinnamon sticks, which provide the base for bay leaf blooms punctuated with anise centers. The grape cluster is made of whole nutmeg kernels and permanent leaves. It's a dramatic but simple display suitable for either a window or tabletop.

Textured collection

An unusual design of massed miniature callas, persimmons, and cockscomb in deep tones fill a ribbed papier-mâché pot, which has been covered with cinnamon sticks. Affixed with pan-melt glue, the cinnamon sticks provide a dramatic, warmly hued base for this impressive design.

krafty columns

Kraft paper columns set a harvest theme

Kraft-paper-covered columns in graduated heights, which are made of foam-centered board, are a perfect fall setting for blooming and green plants. Paper ribbon trims the top of each column, and each pedestal is decorated in an individual style. The taller columns are embellished with faux vegetables: one wears an ear of corn made from yellow-painted foam-centered board with a shuck of paper ribbon and Spanish moss "silk," and the other sports a cauliflower frontispiece made of bleached yarrow with a collar of paper ribbon leaves. The smaller pedestals are decorated with glued-on excelsior and sections of dried squash.

1 Place a yellow-painted, corn-shaped piece of foam-centered board on top of a piece of foam. Draw kernels with black marker.

2 Cover sides of the foam with pieces of green paper ribbon to resemble shucks, overlapping one on top of the other.

3 Finish the edges with Spanish moss to resemble corn silk at the top and near the shuck openings. Attach to column.

Cattails for fall

Spires of cattails are an unmistakable symbol of autumn, and here they are combined in a definitive masculine design of pheasant feathers, seeded *Eucalyptus*, grasses, and blossoms in glowing fall shades.

autumn leaves

Welcome glorious fall with showers of flaming leaves

Welcome fall with showers of burnished leaves to bring the exuberance of the season to your shop window. Attach permanent fabric leaves to strands of copper bullion, and hang them parallel to each other to create the effect of falling leaves. Shiny black buckets hold collections of fabric flowers in blazing fall colors, and one overturned bucket casually scatters more fiery leaves. Stacks of pumpkins, squash, or gourds could also be used to provide more variety to this setting, which will certainly inspire customers to come inside and see what's new.

Leafy touch

Make this vase arrangement sensationally autumn by simple additions. Spray-paint the bottom two inches of the clear vase a warm green tone, then attach autumn leaf stickers, readily available at hobby stores, in a band around the outside of the vessel to hide the paint transition. Add a few sprigs of preserved oak leaves to the mixture of autumn-toned roses and *Dahlias*, and you're done!

rugged southwest

Flaming colors and hot spices tell the story of canyon lands

Sunset colors from a southwestern landscape bring the strength of a primitive land to a bountiful gathering of many textures and earthy tints. Textures abound in natural and dried elements, such as curly ting ting, pods, acorns, quince slices, chili peppers, and dried grasses, which seem to burst from a rustic bark bucket. Potpourri, feathers, and an acorn fill a clay bowl, which has the look of hand-thrown pottery. Other accessories are a background poster in desert canyon hues, textiles with Native American motifs, and mounted greeting cards to carry out the theme of the Southwest's soaring sense of space and powerful mystique.

Southwestern flavors

A great gift basket corrals the tastes and temptations of the Southwest. A darker shade of basket sets off its gourmet components. Tucked in for a bit of added color, strawflowers pick up the colors of the cloth napkin lining the basket.

kraft paper backdrops

Painted kraft paper for simple-to-make displays

Place palm leaves over kraft paper and spray to create a shadowed outline.

Utilitarian kraft paper lends itself to creative backdrops that are quickly made and can be adapted to many themes and seasons. We've chosen to give our kraft paper backdrop the shadowy look and depth of foliage. Select the leaves you want to use; arrange them in a pleasing pattern; and spray with wood-toned and metallic-gold paints. Be sure to leave an unpainted area in the center of the backdrop to pull the eye into the display. Hang the backdrop from the ceiling, and arrange floral designs and accessories in front of it. We've used an unusual topiary arrangement in a rustic wooden container and burled wooden candlesticks set on top of a stack of old books to carry out a subdued, subtle color scheme that would be a perfect transition display between seasons.

Subtle elegance

An earthenware pot showcases lilies and roses. Parsnips, turnips, and wild wheat add a natural contrast to the flowers while a sliced red cabbage provides a grace note to the pink tones. Artichoke and butternut squash further add engaging hues to this soft design.

picket fence charm

Stark white illuminates organic textures

White picket fencing forms a shelving unit filled with a mix of deep greens and many-textured flowers, fruits, and potted plants. Earthen stoneware, wood, terra-cotta, and glazed ceramic provide a plethora of container choices. Potted ornamental kale, a rosemary topiary, poppy pods and apples, artichokes, and *Zinnias* offer varied selections, all in the same vein of country simplicity and organic arrangements. A small stepladder painted white, and a wooden crate, also white, finish a display that yearns for all things natural. Everything here, except the green *Hypericum* berries in the chartreuse urn, are permanent materials that create garden-like, simple-but-durable arrangements for patio or kitchen.

Apple delight

'Golden Delicious' apples, variegated *Pittosporum*, and goldenrod (*Solidago*), in coordinating hues of yellow and green fill a ceramic container that has the aged look of a farm crock. The apples are picked for stability and inserted into floral foam, which is further stabilized by the weight of the heavy container.

textured nature

Natural elements are placed for visual impact

Make a storage area in your shop for display materials, and assemble items by theme for future displays. By planning ahead, you'll always be ready with fresh, new props.

Inexpensive, small, unfinished wood shelves and crates can be used to great advantage as fixtures to create an eye-catching display. Wicker drawers and other small occasional accessories showcase dried and textural products that are timeless in their appeal and that you're likely to carry in your shop year-round. A twig ball provides a focal area display while other dried elements and materials can radiate from that central point. The monochromatic color scheme gives visual importance to each item in the display so that nothing is overlooked.

Harvest gathering

Covered with a sheaf of dried barley and filled with sectioned clusters of fresh flowers and artichokes—a technique that showcases the vegetative types and emphasizes their compelling textures— a papier-mâché pot resembles a decorated bushel basket overflowing with fall's abundant harvest. The gracious composition celebrates the bounty of the season.

happy halloween lights

Light up autumn with a fanciful display

A string of whimsical lights with jack-o-lantern faces sets a seasonal tone. Use this novelty light idea in your front window or in a darker corner inside, where additional light is needed. Since the lanterns are cut from yellow cups, rather than the expected orange, the color is subtle enough to be used throughout the fall season and can be used in many ways to complement seasonal icons such as scarecrows, ghosts, or witches and a natural gathering of decorative gourds and squashes.

1 Cut different styles of faces in inverted party cups with an artist's knife, just as if you were carving a pumpkin face.

2 Make two bisecting cuts in the bottom of each cup, so that a light can be inserted.

3 Unscrew the bulb from each individual light, push the bulb socket through the hole in the cup, then reinsert the bulb.

Bag a halloween design

Fashion a trick-or-treat bouquet by covering a utility vase with a small paper bag. Affix a Halloween sticker or cutout from a holiday card to the bag, and tie it smartly with raffia. Make these by the dozens for inexpensive fall gift giving.

76

it's boo time!

Spooky icons herald Halloween

Scored and folded foam-centered board shapes a delightfully frightful background of harvest moon and black cat for Halloween merchandise and brightly hued *Gerberas* in terra-cotta pots. The humorous witch will attract children, without frightening, and promises a fun goose-bump holiday time for everyone. With a bit of ingenuity and a minimum of skills, a similar scene can be created by hanging Halloween cutouts. The backdrop promises lots of Halloween treats for youngsters and adults and encourages shopping for holiday décor.

Candy corn canister

Cater to a sweet tooth with this color-fully decorated glass canister filled with an old favorite, candy corn. Even the miniature bouquet arranged in a small dome of floral foam, which is adhered to the top of the canister, carries the theme of the candy corn colors—fresh car-nations, spray mums, and goldenrod (*Solidago*) in bright oranges and yellows. Finished with a touch of coordinating ribbon, it's just right for a petite fall gift.

the witching hour

Halloween designs for a spooky evening

Halloween isn't just for children any longer. Adults have made Halloween a very popular holiday for parties, and here's a frightful design that simulates a midnight cemetery visit and sets the mood for a spooky evening. Faux stone paint gives the plastic foam tombstone the look of granite, and adhesive lettering from a sign shop makes the epitaph. Surrounded by orange and violet-colored fresh flowers and branches of winged elm, the design appears to be naturally growing at the base of the stone. Feathered black crows perched atop the stone and in the foliage below add an ominous touch, symbolic of a time when it is believed that spirits walked between the worlds.

1 Cut out a tombstone shape from a 2-inch-thick sheet of plastic foam.

2 Spray the tombstone with Fleckstone® textured paint.

3 Use precut vinyl letters to add an epitaph to the tombstone.

Eerie visitors

A wooden birdhouse provides a perch for somber, realistic crows and brings a mysterious touch to an All Hallows arrangement.

78

graveyard ghosties

Ghostly denizens spark Halloween décor

A skeleton balloon kit and a discarded flower box come together to forge a ghoulishly, goose-bumpy display. The flower box coffin was first spray-painted with silver and then with black to achieve the look of metal, and the skeleton is situated in one end of the coffin, leaving space for the "expired" casket spray of fresh and dried material in the other end. The flowers are accented with mournful black ribbon, and the whole display is ready to bring a few chills to a ghostly evening. Continue this theme inside your store, and spark ideas for Halloween parties by setting an erie Halloween table with an attractive fresh center-piece and more balloon skeletons seated around the party setting.

Ghostly haunts

Ghost-white carnations and cute sponge spooks make delightful vase arrangements to celebrate a spooky holiday. Inexpensive sponge images of ghosts, witches, cats, and other Halloween motifs can be found at craft stores and glued to glass containers for holiday themed designs.

multicolor risers and wraps

Multi-hued risers and containers stimulate sales

When the elements of a display are placed at varying heights, each element receives the customer's undivided attention; at the same time it can be seen how each element coordinates with another. These wooden crate risers have their wooden lath sides painted in coordinating but different colors—orange, lavender, and sienna. Dusky woven baskets and single stems of complementing fabric flowers lend themselves to a pleasing display. Different color themes can be used with the risers simply by changing the painted laths—red and green for Christmas or pastels for spring and Easter. The applications are endless, and with a change of color, the whole display is new again.

Colorful "wraps"

A yard or two of inexpensive craft fabric from your local fabric store can transform utilitarian glass cylinders. Just cut fabric into strips—fabric with a horizontal pattern is best—spray the backsides with adhesive, and carefully wrap the strips around the vases.

fall pumpkin parade

Get ready for fall with a pumpkin vine

For fall, think pumpkins. This pumpkin garland brings the ambience of fall to your window with air-filled latex balloons. For Halloween, add pumpkins with painted faces to the patch; and as you move into November, replace them with corn shocks. By adding Thanksgiving giftware and a cornucopia to the display, it will continue to look new and fresh and with a bit of ingenuity, can span all facets of the fall season.

1 To make the pumpkin vine, inflate orange latex balloons in different sizes.

2 Wrap each balloon with green florist's twine to create the look of a ribbed pumpkin.

3 Tie a single ivy leaf to the balloon knot to complete the pumpkin stem. Attach balloons to an ivy garland.

Petite holiday bouquet

Orange carnations are perfect for a simple and timesaving design for fall or Halloween, which can be used as an individual gift or in multiples for a festive table. To make the pumpkin stem, use a longer stem and glue on a pair of leaves.

cast a spell

Halloween enticements for a spooky evening

Entice Halloween spooks of all ages into your shop to see what's cooking for that spooky holiday with this delightfully witchy character. Poised over her bubbling cauldron of transparent white and black balloons and overflowing Spanish moss, she's stirring with a clutch of twigs as she casts her midnight spells. The witch is easily made from extra-wide paper ribbon; her hair is raffia, and her face and hand are carved from Styrofoam™ and spray-painted green. Though she gives the illusion of depth, she's really two dimensional, and the fire beneath her cauldron is simulated with pieces of plastic film tucked between cut twigs. Since she's simple to assemble, she could be quickly duplicated for holiday parties.

Happy jacks

Cut the bottoms out of party-favor-sized jack-o'-lanterns, and slip them over a cylinder vase to create a happy Halloween container.

happy turkey day

Flowers make a family gathering memorable

In the rush to get everything ready for the Christmas holidays, it's all too easy to overlook Thanksgiving, which is a traditional gathering time for families. Flowers should be an integral part of the food, fun, and frivolity of Turkey Day, so don't let those sales slip away. Try this high-impact yet easily constructed checkerboard pattern to highlight festive floral designs in autumnal tones. The background is created with graphic images of a turkey, which are adhered to pieces of foam-centered board with photo mounting spray adhesive. This specific image, along with an amazing 1,431 others, is available at *www.clipart.com*. Print the turkey image on a color printer and print a black and white version to be photocopied on colored paper. Arrange the images in checkerboard fashion on foam-centered board for a lively Thanksgiving display.

Harvest accents

Small collections of botanicals offer great versatility for consumers and ease of design for florists. Fresh roses and yarrow are inserted in water tubes, which are hidden within the excelsior-filled glass pots. Freeze-dried crab apples, nestled among the florals, give a final autumnal touch to a small design that works well singly or in multiples.

cornucopias—symbols of the season

Turn corrugated material into autumn vignette

Corrugated border material commonly used on school room bulletin boards and above chalkboards is an interesting textured cardboard that is metamorphosed into a jumbo, display-sized cornucopia and matching container. These containers are filled with a mix of permanent pome-granates, crab-apple branches, and bamboo foliage, which accents the earthy color of the corrugated border.

1 Separate a roll of corrugated bulletin board border into two halves width-wise along the perforation. Push the center of the roll out to form a cone shape. Curve the cone into a cornucopia. Spray the inside with adhesive.

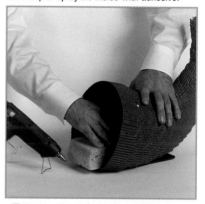

2 Create a base for the cornucopia by hot-gluing a piece of cardboard onto the bottom. Hot-glue plastic foam inside.

Heather horn

Beginning at the end of the cornucopia, place pieces of fresh heather lengthwise around it, wrapping with paddle wire as you work. Cover the entire cornucopia. Then fill it with your choice of autumnal hued blossoms, foliage, or fall fruits and vegetables.

3 Place an 8-inch clay pot on top of the remaining half of the corrugated border roll. Pull it up to cover the pot to the desired height. Fill the pot with foam.

"punkins" and paper bags

Blue denim patched pumpkins

Cut squares of denim to form a "patch" for the fresh pumpkins. Staple in place with a staple gun positioning each staple to resemble hand-sewn stitches.

Pumpkins and patches shout, "Come inside and see what's new!" Use always-popular blue denim with orange, and the complementary color combination will sew up sales. Attach scraps of blue denim—patches—to real pumpkins with spray adhesive, and then staple the patch edges. The staples provide a home-sewn, stitched country look so right for the harvest season. Add containers in a cobalt hue to accent your display, and a large brown paper bag bursting with additional miniature pumpkins and ornamental gourds. Sunflowers and seasonal grasses accent a pleasing display that requires little cash. Put the patched pumpkins in your shop window, and stack some near your entryway to expand the theme throughout your showroom.

Burst of fall

Add excitement to a potted 6-inch chrysanthemum by creating a burst of black bearded wheat around the blossoms and styling a collar of permanent *Magnolia* leaves to base the arrangement in a pewter-toned plastic urn.

harvest icons welcome the season

Permanent pumpkins and gourds top hay bale "topiaries"

Strong yet simple designs create a topiary effect as permanent pumpkins, gourds, and squash cap hay bales, which are placed inside country-style, painted wooden bin containers. Miniature hay bales, available especially for the fall holidays, are turned onto their ends to create a column effect and to give needed height for displaying these smaller items. Permanent *Magnolia* leaves are layered atop the bales where the permanent decoratives sit, and a collar is shaped of the same leaves for the single pumpkin that rests directly on the lip of its container. The hay bales provide added emphasis and could be used with other merchandise such as small flowering plants, or the entire vignette could be incorporated into a much larger-scaled display.

Harvest gathering

A charming collection of seasonal elements captures the feeling of harvest with its multiple textures. A straw bird's nest, housing a single speckled wooden egg, provides a charming focal area for the composition. Add a drop of scented oil for a subtle reminder of the season.

glowing holiday color

Clear glass cylindrical vases glow with vibrant color

For a display that unerringly draws the eye and catches the breath, fill a window with dozens of crystal-clear glass cylinders, each containing a different color of Christmas ball ornament. Use a single color in each container, but pull away from the traditional colors of Christmas and use, instead, chartreuse, fuchsia, orange, and yellow for a color-blocked arrangement. But don't limit yourself to the Christmas holiday only—fill glass containers with hearts for Valentine's Day or pumpkins, pine cones, or colorful permanent fruits for fall. And don't forget flowers! Dropping in a colorful plant or grouping of blossoms would fill these containers with yet another easy-to-create display variation.

Grandiose urn

Dazzling iridescent colors of deep purple, red-violet, chartreuse, and burnt orange spill from this grandly doubled urn, crafted of two artfully combined wire baskets, one hot-glued inside the other.

ribbon, ribbon everywhere

Glorious ribbons are an added enticement

Too often a florist's beautiful ribbons are hidden away in the back room. A display like this one shows your clients ribbons available by the yard. An inexpensive shelving unit and a window sash provide the display fixtures. Both are painted with flat white paint and rubbed with acrylic burnt umber, creating an antique look. The shelf holds bolts of ribbon stacked in varying ways while the window's "panes" are squares of foam-centered board that have been covered with weavings of different styles of ribbon. A ribbon-covered box provides a plant presentation.

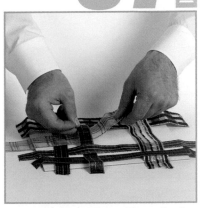

1 Lay out lengths of ribbon, all in one direction, to cover a square of foam-centered board. Weave pieces of ribbon in the opposite direction, one at a time, alternately over and under the first pieces.

2 Fold the ends of each piece of ribbon over the edges of the foam-centered board, and secure them to the back side of the board with hot glue.

3 Press the ribbon-covered squares of foam-centered board into the window openings, and fasten them in place with tape or tiny nails.

Ribbon squared

Squares of cranberry and red velvet ribbon are attached to a plastic foam cone in an overlapping pattern with pearl-headed pins. The result is decidedly contemporary, culminating in a denser pattern of squares and pins near the top of the cone.

88

geometry lessons

Geometric shapes— from simple to complex

For sleek sophistication, fill your window with moss-covered spheres and wreaths. Echoing the minimalist department store display genre, this presentation suggests a multitude of possibilities and jump-starts your customer's creativity, as his mind makes the leap from simple display to luxurious holiday ideas. Hang wreath forms from wide red ribbons for the most impact and to provide a hint of Christmas' traditional red and green. Spheres and wreaths can be held together by wooden picks and secured in containers; gray ones are used here to subtly underscore the green of the shapes. Don't limit yourself to wreaths and spheres; try rectangles, ovals, and cubes as well. Customize the shapes and numbers of items used to the size of your particular shop window.

Circle of roses

"Flame" roses and huckleberry are arranged in a foam ring, and additional rings of copper wire are laid over the huckleberry. Pieces of *Equisetum* fill the inside circumference of the circle, and bear grass clippings, spread in the remaining area of the box, surrounds the circle of roses, creating a textured carpet to the edges of the box.

star light, star bright

Falling stars light up the window

Cut a five-pointed star from a piece of gold mat board. Score the mat board from each point of the star into the center. On the opposite side, score the board from the "intersections" between the points into the center. Fold the star alternately inward and outward along the score lines into a 3-D form.

A quad of falling, golden stars created from mat board make a repeating motif that develops a unified theme for this display. Movement is suggested by two sizes of stars suspended at different levels while two others seem to have come to rest on Earth. The eye follows the line created by the largest star and moves along from star to star, pausing for a moment at a smaller one, which holds a lighted pillar candle. This leads on to the real "star" of the exhibit—florals beautifully arranged in a star-shaped container. The floral arrangement features carnations in lush hues, evergreen, and a final burst of gold foiled stars. Captivating as this display is, its value doesn't stop at merchandising; the idea could also be sold as holiday décor for homes and offices, holiday weddings, and parties.

Light up the holidays

A cheery bunch of fire-engine-red miniature carnations bespeak the joy of the Christmas holidays. Arranged in a clay pot that has been spray-painted wintry white, the garland of Christmas tree lights is made by wrapping beading wire around the bases of the bulbs, then winding the strand around the base of the blossoms. A bit of green ribbon complements the design's foliage.

collected extravagances

Collections of dinnerware and flowers create home décor grandeur

A collection of attractive plates can be used to create a pleasing display that doesn't require a great deal of time or effort to assemble. Hang a collection of collector's plates, or even a collection of vintage porcelain, perhaps with a rose motif. Coordinate a beautiful airy floral design, incorporating the colors, flowers, or motifs of the plates. There are many ways to use this display inside the shop or in the window. Ideally, the plates in the display should come from your shop's giftware, and they could be any style that will showcase your lovely floral arrangements.

Baroque floral

A resurging interest in baroque grandeur is making its appearance in home furnishings, and this towering design would be perfectly at home with such massive furniture. A stately urn is filled with luxurious red velvety roses, seeded *Eucalyptus*, and berries. Glimmery filaments are interwoven throughout, and a *Protea* topped with a burnished finial repeats the metallic container.

magnificent silver

The elegance of silver creates instant impact

The sleek sophistication of silver provides an all-stops-out fanfare for a truly elegant holiday display. An observer's eye could become lost among the many objects shown here if it weren't for the unifying elements of metallic silver and the various-sized glass spheres which are purposefully added in strategic spots throughout the setting. Julep cups are filled with fresh dusty miller and millimeter spheres. Two different sizes of vases are stacked to achieve soaring height and are finished with a silver, artichoke-shaped finial. Another trumpet vase arrangement is topped with an inverted silver tussie-mussie holder while permanent evergreen and preserved foliages offer welcome relief to the eye. An impressive chased silver urn filled with more silvery spheres gives needed weight to balance the display.

Silver topiary

An ivy topiary is aflutter with delicate, silver-painted feather butterflies, and the nickel champagne bucket adds a touch of keepsake elegance. This could be an impressive gift for Mom for the holidays or provide a festive welcome to a holiday party.

bow dangles

Ornaments dance on wreath form "tree"

Get a double-take from customers when they spy this unique display made from mundane wire wreath forms. Spray-painted in metallic gold, ho-hum is left behind as each ring is hung with a variety of light-catching Christmas ornaments in lustrous shades of purple, fuchsia, and gold. Without disturbing the beauty of the display, holiday shoppers can easily choose from a brimming bowl full of the gorgeous tree trimmers, which can be refilled as needed. Our display incorporates 8-inch, 9-inch, 12-inch, and 14-inch rings in the "tree" although you could use fewer rings or other sizes to fit the available space. Fine-gauge chain is evenly spaced and attached to each ring, then secured to a single chain for hanging. A coordinating ribbon bow tops the display.

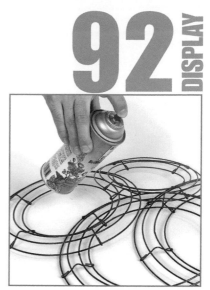

1 Choose an appropriate number of wreath rings in sequential sizes. Paint them gold.

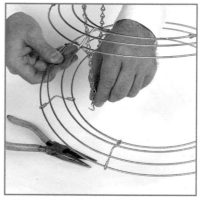

2 Connect the rings using four strands of chain. Open the needed links with pliers, hook them to the rings, and close the links.

3 Hang an assortment of ornaments from the rings using coordinating ribbon. Tie bows to the rings for decoration.

Candle creation

An elegantly simple candle design utilizes a ball candle and a silver mint julep cup. A diminutive wreath of heather (*Erica*) created with beading wire and wrapped with a crystal beaded garland surrounds the clear saucer, where the candle rests.

93

christmas "tree" merchandising

Sumptuous ribbon and fabric ornaments in perfect display

An impressive Christmas "tree" display provides an unusual setting to show wonderfully crafted Christmas ornaments. The tree is created with foam-centered board that is spray-painted gold, and its different levels provide ample space to hang and to place glowing velvet and brocade ornaments embellished with bits of golden cord, braid, tassels, and ribbon. Lengths of golden, French-wired ribbon are used to visually connect and unify the graduated levels of the tree. It easily breaks down for storage and can be used from year to year. The rich, deep colors of the ornaments create the ambiance of a Russian royal court and are sure to provide a unique choice for the customer looking for something different in holiday trims.

Ribbon vase

Here a utilitarian glass vase is covered with rich fabric ribbon and enhanced with brocaded ribbon, golden cord, and a golden ribbon rose. Both the vase and the sphere provide a touch of regal elegance wherever they're placed.

sugarplum dreams

Turn an empty flower box into a candied holiday scene

Create a holiday scene evocative of "The Night Before Christmas" with a bed made of a discarded flower box decorated with candies. It's guaranteed to get little ones and adults into the holiday spirit with happy remembrances. A doll tucked beneath a snowy coverlet along with a teddy bear, childhood toys, and a book or two bring back memories and inspiration for the holidays.

1 Swirl red ribbon, equally spaced, around the length of four white poster tubes. Affix gumdrops between the ribbon strips, and attach a plastic foam ball to the end of each tube.

2 Cut an appropriate shape from foam-centered board to form the bed boards and the rug. Create the rug by adhering rows of candy onto the board.

3 Attach the ends and posts to a discarded flower box. Use cotton batting to make a pillow and blanket.

Peppermint possibilities

Festive with peppermint candies and candy-striped mini carnations, this joyful arrangement speaks volumes about the holiday season. The peppermint stick house glued to the side of the clear glass container emphasizes the candy-striped theme.

christmas gingerbread house

A garage sale find is transformed

A gently used garage sale dog house—cleaned and freshly painted tan—becomes the much beloved gingerbread house of the Christmas holidays. Shredded wheat cereal segments are glued to the roof to create shingles while the roof apex is decorated with alternating rounds of candy drops and peppermint. "Frosting" made from hot glue drips from the eaves, and candy sticks are glued end-to-end at the corner edges of the house. Jelly beans and other candies outline the door opening while spiraled lollipops imitate shrubbery. Crushed plastic foam creates the look of fluffy snow scattered about the house, and flat lozenge candies create the walkway to complete this idyllic scene. An afternoon spent decorating this little house yields a display that can be stored and used again and again.

Hand-dipped chocolate

A yummy design of faux delectable treats fill a "chocolate" pot to bursting. Create the chocolate-covered container by dipping a clay pot in melted pan glue. Then place the pot on plastic wrap sprayed with cooking spray, and apply several coats of brown spray paint.

the splendor of gold

Golden ribbons create a dazzling display

Gold and gold-accented ribbons used in a bevy of ways simply take the breath away. Nothing is more luxurious or elegant than the stunning impact of gold. Use it for Christmas décor, but use it for weddings and anniversaries, too. Its appeal is timeless. Here are some wonderful ways with golden ribbons—a lovely pomander made of freeze-dried roses and shimmery ribbon; a sphere wrapped with gold ribbon, embellished with cording, and set atop a candlestick to create a striking topiary; and a utilitarian glass vase turned glamorous with the addition of festive ribbons.

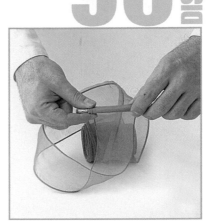

1 Tightly wrap several layers of wired ribbon around a pencil. A sheer organza or chiffon works best.

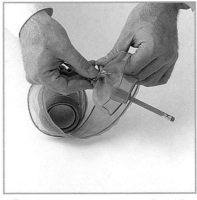

2 Continue wrapping the pencil, adding folded pleats at the bottom and causing the top of the ribbon to flare.

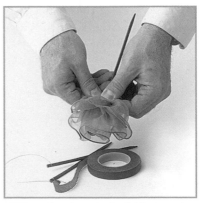

3 To create a stem, wire the finished rose to a wired wood pick and wrap with florists' tape.

Ribbon roses

Lavish in appearance but simple to make, a ribbon rose makes a statement wherever it's used. Make them from wired satin or organza ribbons; different types of ribbon lend a different "look" to the rose.

97

yesteryear designs

Nostalgic designs for vintage décor

With the current interest in all things Victorian and vintage, take advantage of the trend, and create a little corner of yesterday in your shop. Bring back warm memories with antique replica toys, ornaments, a teddy bear, wooden trays, and baskets. The luxurious wreath combines velvet fruit and flowers, cones, and miniature toys while the coordinating handled wooden basket is filled with similar materials and a hand-crocheted doily. A smaller rectangular basket arrangement is wrapped up in sheer ribbon and accented with a doily, too, for a thoughtful gift. The garland of balls covered with beans, corn, and peas is a homey touch that works well with the darker tones of home décor from a bygone era. Stoppered apothecary jars filled with potpourri are reminiscent, too, of another time.

Vintage vignette

Jackie berries, which are dried, and dyed seed heads cover this wreath, creating an unusual texture for such a design. Simple yet contemporary, this thin composition is perfect for a narrow space, such as between a front door and a screen door.

christmas kitchen

A tempting holiday kitchen display

During the holiday season, the family kitchen becomes the heart of the home as seasonal goody-baking gets underway. Kitchen-themed products have been found to sell well by florists, and it is certainly a fitting way to display those wonderful cookie-like ornaments and other holiday kitchen ceramics such as cookie jars and teapots. Although these "cookie" ornaments could certainly be displayed on a small tree, this innovative little shelf provides a perfect backdrop that highlights the ornaments and other holiday kitchen merchandise. By creating a space to display these ornaments away from a tree, the shopper will be pulled to their fanciful designs. Add a scented candle that wafts the fragrance of baking chocolate chip cookies or plum pudding, and voilà! This holiday "kitchen" becomes irresistible!

Countrified Christmas

Serve up cookie Christmas ornaments on a baking sheet garnished with a country calico patch-and-button topiary and a coordinated basket filled with evergreens and bright, shiny apples. This is Christmas décor your customer will be sure to take home for the holidays.

wintry wonderland

Cellophane icicles and snowy trees set winter scene

An icy wintry window vignette kicks off the cool season and inspires seasonal sales. Plastic foam cones are turned into trees with a shaping slash of the knife. Slivers carved from the sides are glued into pointed tips for the tops of the trees, and white painted dowels make sturdy trunks to hold the white cones aloft in their white ceramic pots. A premade snowman anchored to a snowflake could be one you've created yourself or an ornamental figurine put to use in this snow scene. The *pièce de résistance* in this winter wonderland are the frosty icicles of heat-treated, crinkled cellophane that set a chilly blizzard tone to the display.

1 Roll a piece of cellophane into a cone shape, and wrap a white chenille stem around the larger end of the cone.

2 Staple the edges of the cellophane together so it will hold its cone shape when heated.

3 Holding to the chenille stem, warm the cellophane with a heat gun, shaping as desired.

Winter bubble design

A perfectly contained design for colder weather, the paperwhite (*Narcissus*) blossoms snuggle inside a clear glass bubble bowl. A swirl of artfully placed lily grass (*Liriope*) gracefully lines the sides of the bowl encircling the flowers, and an elegant silvery beaded orb highlights this coolly sophisticated design.

DISPLAY 100 partridges and pears

Twelve Days of Christmas inspires a design that fills a window

Sometimes an elaborate arrangement can fill a window as a complete display. Here the time-honored art of espaliering lends itself to an airy window display created from canes of bamboo and permanent fruits. Pears are the repeating motif on the bamboo grate and in the wooden window box container at the base. A pair of partridges nestles among an abundant assortment of fruit, cones, and fragrant evergreens, which is accented with a few golden pots. The wooden container provides weight for the display, and the lush display heightens the anticipation of the holiday. A collection of holiday fruit baskets, pear-themed gift items, or other gifts with the "Twelve Days of Christmas" theme would fit well with this seasonal display.

Partridge haven

A profusion of unique candle holders has captured the partridge's attention as he rests among a collection of pears, evergreens, and magnolias. A metal urn and a hurricane globe are softened with permanent leaves. A third candle, settled in a twig basket, is surrounded by permanent pears, foliages, and *Alstroemeria* blossoms.

101

decoupaged drama

Victorian decorative technique adds flair

Elegant containers utilize an old technique of scissoring bits of botanical prints or other attractive paper scraps and gluing them on objects for decorative emphasis. Our galvanized metal flower bucket and watering can are spray-painted black, their copper rims unpainted, so the bright metallic edges add unexpected brilliance to the dark intensity of the finished containers. We used fruit prints to continue the fruited motif of the arrangements — delectable combinations of grapes, apples, peaches, and pears.

Fruited hatboxes

Fruit-themed papier-mâché hatboxes are ideal to showcase your shop's gift wrapping capabilities or to use as decorative accents. The boxes are inexpensive and readily available at craft stores, and they don't require any treatment other than the fruit toppers.